C000026134

ANDALUCÍA
including SEVILLE

BY
JOHN GILL WITH NICK INMAN

Produced by
Thomas Cook Publishing

Written and updated by John Gill with Nick Inman
Original photography by Michelle Chaplow
Original design by Laburnum Technologies Pvt Ltd

Editing and page layout by Cambridge Publishing
Management Ltd, Unit 2, Burr Elm Court,
Caldecote CB3 7NU
Series Editor: Karen Beaulah

Published by Thomas Cook Publishing
A division of Thomas Cook Tour Operations Ltd
Company Registration No. 1450464 England

PO Box 227, The Thomas Cook Business Park,
Unit 18, Coningsby Road,
Peterborough PE3 8SB, United Kingdom
E-mail: books@thomascook.com
www.thomascookpublishing.com
Tel: +44 (0) 1733 416477

ISBN: 978-1-84157-706-7

First edition © 2003 Thomas Cook Publishing
Second edition © 2007 Thomas Cook Publishing

Project Editor: Linda Bass
Production/DTP Editor: Steven Collins

Printed and bound in Italy by: Printer Trento.

Cover design by: Liz Lyons Design, Oxford.
Front cover credits: Left © Thomas Cook; centre © Massimo Ripani/4 Corners;
right © Glen Allison/Alamy
Back cover credits: Left © Thomas Cook; right © Thomas Cook

The people

Given its history, Andalucía could claim to be the most ethnically diverse region in Europe. Since at least a thousand years before recorded history, it has been receiving settlers and invaders from all four sides. The Phoenicians, Carthaginians and Romans mixed with the indigenous prehistoric farming populations they found. The Moors from North Africa left a profound mark from the 8th century on, as later did Hispano-Americans coming from Spain's colonies across the Atlantic. More recently, Andalucía has become a magnet for people from northern Europe looking for a home in the sun, and for immigrants from sub-Saharan Africa and Eastern Europe in search of any work they can find. Andalucía sometimes struggles to accommodate such different social groups, but compared to the rest of Europe it remains a markedly tolerant place.

Sunflowers are one of Andalucía's most picturesque crops

History

30,000 BC(?)	Estimated age of palaeolithic cave drawings found in La Cueva de Pileta, Montejaque, Serrania de Ronda mountains.
15,000–7000 BC	Spread of farming and settlements begins to overtake hunter-gatherer cultures, spreading from the Fertile Crescent (modern-day Middle East) westwards.
4000 BC	Burial mound in Granada province from this date contained clothing, including shoes, religious offerings and other gifts. At roughly the same time, animal husbandry or cattle breeding begins.
2200 BC	Bronze Age artefacts from this period found in dolmen burial chambers at Millares, Almeria.
1100 BC	Founding of Cádiz, said to be Europe's first city, by Phoenician adventurers on lagoon at mouth of Rio Guadalete (Guadalete River).
600 BC	Greek traders arrive on Mediterranean coast, likely importers of earliest olive trees.
500 BC	Carthage colonises southern part of peninsula.
206 BC	Romans defeat Carthaginians, begin construction of Italica (5km/3 miles north of modern Seville).
AD 415	Visigoths from northern Europe's modern-day Baltic regions invade Spain.
446	Spain under Visigoth control.
590	First Visigoth conversions to Christianity.
711	Tariq ibn Zayid, governor of Tangier, lands a 10,000-strong Berber army near Tarifa.
756	Independent Moorish emirate declared in Córdoba.
1085	First decisive victory of Catholic Reconquest at Toledo.
1147	Almohads take Seville and regions, begin construction of Torre del Oro and Giralda tower.
1236	Christians retake Córdoba.

1248	Christians retake Seville.	**1630**	Madrid overtakes Seville as the largest city in Spain.
1469	Marriage of Fernando of Aragon and Isabel of Castilla unites the kingdoms of Castilla and Aragon. Fernando and Isabel prosecute the Reconquest with vigour.	**1701–13**	War of the Spanish Succession in which the Habsburg kings are supplanted by the Bourbon dynasty through the invervention of France.
1480	Inquisition established in Seville. Among its first victims are homosexuals, Jews and, later, protestants and Mudéjars (Moors who were 'allowed to stay').	**1713**	Under the Treaty of Utrecht, Britain takes control of Gibraltar.
1492	The last Moorish redoubt, Granada, falls to the Christians. Columbus sails for the Americas funded by the Spanish throne.	**1717**	With the Rio Guadalquivir silted and no longer navigable, trade with the Americas moves to Cádiz.
1519	Hernán Cortés conquers Peru.	**1804–14**	Peninsular War (called the War of Independence in Spain) in which British troops under Wellington fight with the Spanish to drive invading French troops out of Spain. At the Battle of Bailen (Jaén) in 1808, Napoleon suffers defeat at the hands of a Spanish army. Cádiz is besieged by the French but holds out.
1532	Ferdinand Magellan embarks on the first circumnavigation of the world.		
1580	Seville is officially declared the largest city in Spain.		
1588	Spanish Armada launches an attack on England but is defeated in the English Channel.	**1805**	Britain defeats the combined fleets of Spain and France at the Battle of Trafalgar off Cabo Trafalgar (Cape Trafalgar), north of Tarifa.
1609	King Felipe III orders expulsion of all Moors from Spain.		

1811–12	Spanish radicals establish the Cortes, or Spanish Parliament, in Cádiz, under a state of siege. The liberals are defeated by Bourbon king Fernando VII but set a template for a future constitution.
1833	Disputes between conservative Fernando VII and liberal Carlos IV lead to the First Carlist War.
1835	Church property confiscated and sold off.
1846	Second Carlist War.
1872	Third (and final) Carlist War.
1873	Shortlived First Republic established, but founders due to inability to control Spain's regions. Monarchy restored in 1874.
1881	Pablo Picasso born in Málaga.
1882	Worsening conditions for farm workers in western Andalucía, in particular around Seville, lead to increasing unrest.
1895–8	Spain loses Cuba during the US-backed Cuban War.
1910	La Confederación Nacional del Trabajo (National Labour Confederation, or CNT) founded in Seville by embryonic anarchists following Russian theorists such as Mikhail Bakunin.
1917	Start of three years of anarchist uprising across Andalucía.
1923	General Miguel Primo de Rivera stages military coup, winning support with promises to modernise state and economy.
1929	The great Ibero-American Exposition coincides with the Wall Street Crash (30 November).
1930	Effects of the Depression unseat Rivera, who is replaced in 1931 by a new Second Republic, one riven by factional dispute.
1936	Tensions between the right-wing Falange and the disorganised left-wing Popular Front break out into open Civil War.
1939	The Civil War ends with defeat for the left. Franco keeps Spain out of the

Second World War, but
Spain is boycotted by the
United Nations, forcing
the nation, Andalucía
particularly, into *los años
de hambre* (Years of
Hunger), during which
many starve.

1947	Bullfighter Manolete is killed at Linares.
1969	Gibraltar border closed.
1975	Franco's death brings about the end to his absolute dictatorship. Franco favourite Bourbon Juan Carlos becomes King Juan Carlos I and seizes moment to modernise Spain's democracy and economy.
1982	El Partido Socialista Obrero Español (Spanish Socialist Workers' Party, PSOE, led by Felipe Gonzalez) is voted into power.
1982	Andalucía becomes an autonomous region governed from Seville.
1985	Border with Gibraltar opened after 16-year blockade.
1986	Spain joins the European Community.

1992	Expo 92 puts Seville and Spain back on the world stage.
1996	After 14 years of PSOE government, Spain elects the centre-right Partido Popular (PP), led by former tax inspector José María Aznar.
2002	Peseta is replaced by euro as the official currency.
2004	Terrorist bombs planted on trains travelling into Madrid indirectly lead to a change of government, and the return to power of the Socialist party under José Luis Rodriguez Zapatero.
2006	Corruption scandal in Marbella shocks Spain. The mayor and many town councillors are arrested for allegedly accepting bribes in return for granting planning permission to property developers.
2006	Tripartite talks between Spain, Britain and Gibraltar agree measures for greater cross-border co-operation, including shared use of the airport.

For centuries after the Reconquest of the Iberian peninsula by Christian armies, Andalucía felt ambivalent about the era that had done most to mark its landscapes, its cities and its culture – the six and a half centuries of rule by the Muslim peoples from North Africa (collectively known as the Moors). Christianity had proved its military superiority and did its best to belittle or destroy the civilisation it had conquered. But despite all the mosques that were converted into churches – most conspicuously Seville's cathedral and what became the Great Mosque in Córdoba – some of Moorish Spain's greatest glories, both material and intangible, have proved enduring and today are given the respect and appreciation they deserve.

In the Andalucían countryside, the Moors laid an agricultural foundation without which much of the region would have remained scrubby desert. Without agriculture, neither the Moors nor their Christian successors could have fed, clothed or financed the villages and towns that in turn supported Seville and other cities.

One of the Moors' chief contributions to Spain was intellectual. Over the several centuries and eras of Moorish rule, they introduced medicine, mathematics, philosophy and law, among other disciplines. In the 12th century Córdoba alone produced the philosopher and physician Averroës (1126–88) and the Jewish philosopher, jurist and physician rabbi Moses ben Maimon, more commonly known as Maimonides (1135–1204), the 'father' of modern medicine.

The Moors' most notable contribution was architectural, although few

contemporary citizens would have had access to these ornate marvels. As well as the great palaces at Seville, Granada and Córdoba, they built lesser but no less exquisite monuments at Medina Azahara, Ronda, and the *alcazabas* (fortresses) at Almería and Málaga.

As well as slipping unobtrusively into the Andalucían and Spanish gene pool, the Moors had a profound effect on Spain and its neighbours to the north. Just as Averroës translated Aristotle and introduced his thinking to western Europe, so other Moorish thinkers and teachers built a bridge between the eastern Mediterranean and western Europe, at a time when western Europe was still mired in the Dark Ages.

Centuries of history written by northern European historians interpreted the Reconquest as an honourable campaign to rid Spain of barbarians, although today it might be seen more as ethnic cleansing. (On the subject of cleansing, it might also be added that the Moors, with their elaborate *hammams* or baths, showed unwashed Europe where the soap was.) Yet it seems that the Moors lived alongside Christians and Jews as amicably as any medieval cultures might, and practised a tolerance notably absent in the attitudes of the Christian victors of the Reconquest. Certainly, Ferdinand and Isabel gave the Inquisition free rein to persecute anyone – first the Moors, then Protestants and Jews, then Moors who had converted to Christianity – whose beliefs and practices were at odds with Catholicism.

The pendulum of historical analysis, literature and popular culture has now swung more towards an idealisation or romanticisation of the Moorish period and there has been an attempt by some modern writers to paint it as a Golden Age of Spanish history, more glorious than the age of the (Christian) empire that followed it. In reality, Islamic Spain was never a simple, homogeneous phenomenon, but a complex era that may have produced great art and advances in learning but also contributed its share of war and civil strife to Spanish history.

Above: The façade of the Alcàzar in Seville
Left: Moorish architecture – Córdoba's magnificent Mezquita

Governance

Any European country where, as recently as 1981, factions in the military thought they could incite a coup by holding its parliament hostage has to have an interesting political history.

Andalucía's parliament

The coup attempt of 23 February 1981 led by Colonel Antonio Tejero Molina was both a test and a proof of Spain's brand new (1977) democracy. Tejero and his men held the Cortes, or parliament, hostage for 24 hours before surrendering. Interestingly, the man responsible for the coup's failure was King Juan Carlos I, who had used Franco's death as an opportunity to usher in a new, modernising democracy. Tejero's rebels, controlled by shadowy figures higher up the armed forces hierarchy, claimed that Carlos supported the coup. When the king informed the country's top generals that he opposed the coup, it fell apart.

The green and white Andalucían flag

While disturbing at the time, the attempted coup proved to most Spanish people that their young democracy was robust enough to withstand armed insurrection.

For centuries, a grotesque imbalance of wealth and power undermined any attempts to stabilise Spanish politics. The advent of *latifundismo*, the distribution of great tracts of land to cronies after the Reconquest, only intensified the disparity, especially in Andalucía, which was the largest and most agricultural of all Spain's regions.

Even the 'Golden Age' of global conquest and trade did little more than enrich the already wealthy, and perhaps ease the appearance of a new, educated middle class. It took revolution and the industrialisation of northern Europe to suggest different models of politics.

Spain watched the French Revolution (1789–99) with interest. Spanish radicals attempted to establish a liberal constitution in Cádiz in 1812, only for it to be quashed by Fernando VII. It was the knock-on effect of industrialisation in northern Europe – negligible in Andalucía, but Barcelona's cotton trade rivalled Manchester's in the mid-19th century – that set in motion the forces that would transform Spain.

Ronda's monument to Blas Infante, founder of the Andalucísmo independence movement

Social unrest began to spread across southern Spain in the mid-19th century, despite failed attempts at republican government. In 1923 General Primo de Rivera launched a military coup, and his junta would rule until 1930. In 1931 the Second Republic was established, prompting the far right to launch the Falange two years later. Increasing tensions between the two sides broke out into Civil War, with General Franco becoming head of state in 1936. Spain remained under his dictatorship until his death in 1975.

By 1982, less than seven years after Franco's death, Spain had become a parliamentary democracy with extensive powers devolved to its regions. Andalucía is one of the 17 *comundidades autonomas* (autonomous regions) into which the country is now divided, with its own government (the Junta de Andalucía) based in Seville. The region is subdivided into eight provinces around the major cities (Almeria, Cadiz, Córdoba, Granada, Huelva, Jaén, Málaga and Seville). Unlike the Basques and Catalans in the north, Andalucíans have a relatively weak sense of their collective identity and the closest they have ever come to having an independence movement was during the Second Republic, immediately before the Civil War, when reformer Blas Infante (1885–1936) called for Andalucía to have more say over its own affairs – a demand that many people would say is largely met by the present system of devolution.

Culture

Flamenco may be the most conspicuous and ubiquitous performance art form in Andalucía, but there's a lot more by way of entertainment and culture in the region if you are willing to look for it. To begin with there is a rich calendar of traditional fiestas, many with their roots in pre-Christian times. As for contemporary art, the cities of southern Spain are on the major concert and exhibition circuits of Europe, and there is a growing sense of Andalucía discovering and elaborating on its own cultural heritage, particularly anything and everything to do with the Moors.

Dancing a *sevillana*

The cultural influence of Andalucía

This culture has produced or been adopted by numerous painters – not least Velázquez, Picasso, Zurbarán, Goya and Murillo – and writers – famously, poets Federico Garcia Lorca, Luis Cernuda and Antonio Machado, and earlier figures such as Tirso de Molina (author of the original *Don Juan*) and peripatetic legend Cervantes. It has also been adopted by contemporary figures such as novelist Juan Goytisolo, and has attracted a lengthy queue of others ready to pledge their *afición* (fondness) for the region,

Carnaval balladeers

not least Washington Irving and Prosper Mérimée (creator of Carmen).

Music and dance

As well as producing Cádiz's favourite musical son, Manuel de Falla, Seville and its regions also gave the world two legends of classical and flamenco guitar, Andres Segovia and Paco de Lucia, not to mention dancer Cristina Hoyos.

The thriving university cities, most notably Seville itself, Granada and Cádiz, have generated an energetic youth culture, particularly since *la movida*, 'the movement', swept away the restrictions of the Franco era in the early 1980s. A noisy underground has produced post-punk and electro bands such as Largartija Nick and Los Planetas, and perhaps uniquely across Europe, Andalucían nightclubs and concerts segue between contemporary dance culture and traditional flamenco and other indigenous folk and popular styles, with audiences displaying equal enthusiasm for both.

Perhaps because Andalucía sits at a junction between three continents, north African, eastern Mediterranean and Central/South American influences are often as recognisable as those from northern Europe or the United States in Spanish popular music. This mixture might best be heard in the work of cult 'world' music band Radio Tarifa. And again perhaps uniquely in European popular music, this is popular music sung in the band's own language.

The home of flamenco (*see p18*) has long had an aversion to the North American invention, jazz, but in recent decades it has produced world-class jazz musicians such as the late Tete Montoliu. Of a newer generation, Seville's Chano Domingo is just one Andalucían who has translated to the world circuit, and contemporary flamenco giant Enrique Morente (*see p19*) makes frequent sorties into the world of jazz. Seville, Granada and Cádiz all have annual festivals that span many of the arts, and some hold specialist jazz or ethnic music festivals.

Seville's world-class Maestranza opera house

Fiestas

Every city, town and village has at least one traditional fiesta a year, invariably centring on some day of religious significance and involving rituals in the church and often processions in the streets. Every fiesta is, in effect, a celebration of local culture in its widest definition. The programme is likely to include folk dancing, arts events and other spectacles, and communal meals to taste local foods and wines. Easter Week (*see pp38–9*) is the busiest fiesta week in the calendar. Other important fiestas in Andalucía are listed on pages 20–21.

Hooded *nazarenos* at Easter

Flamenco

Flamenco, the archetypal Andalucían musical form that for many *is* the sound of Spain, has long been in dire need of demystifying, nowhere more so than in the matter of those castanets. These should be followed swiftly by the gaudy polka-dot gypsy dresses that Spanish women wear to dance the *sevillana*, in turn often mistaken as the 'authentic' flamenco dance.

All of the above 'customs' are almost wholly alien phenomena grafted on to flamenco in the 20th century, much to the anguish of some of flamenco's more traditionalist performers and *aficionados*.

Few histories of flamenco will agree on its origin. Many will concur that it took root among the East European Roma, or gypsy, population who arrived in Spain in the 18th century. Some go back further, to the 15th century and the transition of Arabic folk from the lute to the guitar. Others point to the fascinating recurrence of song forms, themes and instrumentation among folk musics around the Mediterranean littoral. Some even track flamenco back to Roman times.

What all historians agree on, however, is how difficult it can be to hear the real thing today. Flamenco's seed-bed, the cafés, bars and clubs of 19th-century Seville and Jerez, gave way to a commercialised entertainment, the *tablao* (show, or tableau), at the turn of the 20th century. Even the once notorious flamenco caves of the gypsy Sacromonte area of Granada became tourist attractions, with the result that the *gitanos* tended to keep their (usually ad hoc) celebrations to themselves and their friends. It requires a certain detective work, or at least reliable contacts, to locate bona fide flamenco today.

The fundament of flamenco is the vocal form known as *cante jondo* ('deep song'), originally and often today unaccompanied, apart from hand percussion. It is here that we locate the essence of flamenco, *duende* (meaning 'spirit'). Like swing, or the blues, *duende*

is an unquantifiable spirituality glimpsed fleetingly during a performance of great passion. It is most commonly found at *gitano juergas*, private parties, and is as likely to be produced by the joint effects of liquor and cocaine as the muse. The greatest *cantaor* (male singer) of the 20th century, El Camarón, died from excesses of drink and drugs aged 40 in 1992.

Danzas or *bailes* (both meaning 'dances') soon began to accompany the *cante jondo*, as did regional variants such as the *fandango* from Cádiz and the *malagueña* from Málaga. Similarly, the *sevillana* was a medieval country dance appropriated by flamenco.

While traditionalists bemoan the commercialisation of flamenco, the spirit of *duende* has moved on, and probably into the hands of a performer such as Enrique Morente. Morente has pushed the envelope of flamenco more than anyone, producing flamenco masses, working with improvising jazz groups, even delving into electronics and avant-garde sound with bands such as fellow Granadinos Largartija Nick.

Inevitably, flamenco has crossed over with rock and dance music, to the chagrin of purists. Yet to anyone who has observed the dissipation of other Mediterranean folk musics, such as Greek *syrtaki*, the success of bands such as Ketama and Radio Tarifa suggests that Spain's young are maintaining a powerful link with tradition that has simply been abandoned elsewhere.

Flamenco is as popular now as it ever was

Festivals and events

Most of the important events in the calendar of Andalucía are fiestas that are religious in origin, but there are also many arts festivals, often sponsored by regional or local government. *Ferias* (fairs) that began as livestock markets have since become grand social occasions, where the object is to dress up, be with people, to see and be seen.

Carnaval goers in Cádiz

Easter, the biggest event of the year (*see pp38–9*), sets the date for Carnaval which falls in February or March immediately before Lent, and for Whitsuntide (or Pentecost) and Corpus Christi (both of which fall between mid-May and mid-June). If you are thinking of attending one of the grand events of the Andalucían year, either book well in advance – hotels fill up at inflated prices – or stay somewhere not too far away where you can get the occasional rest from the noise and hullabaloo.

Christmas lights in Seville's backstreets

Fiesta de San Anton
16 January, Huéscar
Massive firework display with a celebration of local cuisine.
16–17 January, El Ejido, Almería
Processions culminate in a vast bonfire.
Carnaval
February
Cádiz's Carnaval is the largest in mainland Spain, with parades and costumes. Most communities celebrate, although at a slightly more sedate pitch.
Semana Santa (Holy Week)
From late March to late April
Almost everywhere in Andalucía celebrates Holy Thursday and Good Friday with solemnity and Easter Sunday with jubilation. Seville is famous for its Easter Week processions, but there are also good ones to see in Granada and Málaga.
Feria de Abril (April Fair)
Late April
Immediately after Holy Week, Seville stages a week-long party in flamenco dress in a showground across the river from the city centre.
Cruzes de Mayo
Early May, Córdoba
Competition for the best floral decorations in the old town.

National Festival of Flamenco
Every three years (2007, 2010), Córdoba
One of the biggest flamenco festivals in
Spain, followed by Córdoba's fair and
bullfighting festival.

Feria de Patios
First week in May, Córdoba
The old town opens its domestic patios.

Feria del Caballo
Mid-May, Jerez de la Frontera
Traders descend on the oldest country
event and biggest animal fair in
Andalucía.

Romería El Rocio
Whitsun week, El Rocio
The most famous religious pilgrimage in
Andalucía, in which up to half a million
pilgrims converge on this small town to
celebrate its miraculous icon of the
Virgin.

Corpus Christi
May or June, Zahara de la Sierra
Zahara celebrates by cladding the entire
town centre in living greenery for just
one day.

Romería de los Gitanos
Mid-June, Cabra
Major *gitano* pilgrimage to the shrine of
the Virgen de la Sierra.

Seville's elegant Museo de Bellas Artes

Candelas de San Juan
23 June, Vejer de la Frontera
Bonfires and a giant pyrotechnic bull
illuminate this white village.

**Festival Internaciónal de Música y
Danza de la Cueva de Nerja**
July
Month-long festival of classical and
popular concerts by world-class
performers in the town's remarkable
cave system.

Fiesta de la Virgen del Carmen
*16 July, Marbella and elsewhere on the
coast*
Images of the Virgin are carried in
procession in decorated fishing boats.

Exaltación al Rio Guadalquivir
*Last two weekends in August, Sanlúcar de
Barrameda*
Dramatic horse races, said to date back
thousands of years, along a low-tide
track on the beach, with landward
celebrations in this town famed for its
seafood and manzanilla sherry.

La Goyesca
First week in September, Ronda
Ronda's autumn fair closes with the
Goyesca bullfight, fought in the
costumes shown in Goya's paintings of
bullfighting scenes.

Ferias
August–September
Towns across Andalucía celebrate
colourful fairs, often staggered to allow
towns to visit each other's festivities. Two
of the biggest are in Granada and Málaga.

Wine Harvest Festivals (Vendimia)
September and October
Andalucía's wine producing towns
celebrate the gathering of the grapes and
the making of the year's wine. The biggest
festival is in Jerez de la Frontera.

Impressions of Andalucía

It can take patience to get around and get things done in Andalucía, but slowing down to fit into the pace of local life is not necessarily a bad thing. The region has a good transport infrastructure making it easy to travel about, and if you get lost people will be only too willing to point you in the right direction. Arriving in a new town by whatever means, invariably a good policy is to head for the *plaza mayor* or main square and get your bearings. The tourist information office is likely to be close by.

Seville's café culture

Getting around Seville

Although an important city, Seville is not a large place. The city centre is small enough to negotiate on foot, with a compact if often labyrinthine street layout, and in the main sightseeing area of Santa Cruz you can often walk faster than the traffic. In fact, strolling around Seville (and even getting mildly lost) is one of the pleasures of a visit. Only if you want to explore Triana, the Isla de la Cartuja or the more distant parts of the Parque Maria Luisa will you need to take a bus or taxi. Fortunately, wherever you are in central Seville, there are always two handy landmarks to refer to: the cathedral's Giralda tower rising above all other city roofs, and the Guadalquivir River.

When to go

Spring and autumn are usually the best times to visit Andalucía, although a run of El Niño summers has unbalanced the traditional pattern of clement springs and autumns, ferociously hot summers and temperate winters. It can be balmy in mid-winter and unexpectedly rainy in high summer, although droughts are a regular occurrence throughout Andalucía.

Easter's *Semana Santa*, or holy week, and to a lesser extent the subsequent April Fair, require stamina, a plump purse or wallet and military planning especially in Seville but to some extent also in the other cities. Hotels book up as much as six months in advance, room prices can triple and some central hotels are so close to the round-the-clock celebrations that sleep is out of the question.

Summers can be so hot that day-tripper traffic actually withers back until the autumn, making this a good time to visit if you can handle the heat.

Otherwise spring, which can begin as early as February, is the ideal time to visit although late autumn and even mid-winter can surprise with mild, sunny and even hot days – but be prepared for the rains that keep Andalucía so fertile. Layers of clothing for hot days and cool nights are best, and a light waterproof is always good insurance.

The capital has rail links across Europe

Driving

If you are on a tight schedule or you want to follow your nose to remote places and take your own time, you will need a car to get about. Andalucía has a superb network of motorways linking its major cities and some good main roads too, but minor roads are variable and occasionally you'll find yourself on a bumpy back road that hasn't been repaired for decades.

If you are travelling by car, it's wise to avoid entering cities where parking is likely to be difficult. If you have to, plan ahead by choosing a hotel with a secure car park or finding out about multi-storey car parks near to where you want to go. It also makes sense not to drive into small villages because their narrow street patterns were never designed to allow cars to pass easily. Instead, park on the outskirts and walk in. Wherever you park your car, make sure you leave nothing visible at all inside it that may

tempt someone to break in to see what else there is.

Although some drivers may flout the signs and lines of the highways, that doesn't mean there is no highway code and the police can be quick to penalise errant motorists, often with on-the-spot fines. Speed limits, unless otherwise indicated, are 50kph (30mph) in built-up areas, 90kph (55mph) on roads outside towns and 120kph (75mph) on motorways. Beware of meeting a STOP sign where you might reasonably expect a 'Give Way', and of traffic lights following each other so that you go through a green light but are stopped immediately by a red one.

For more information on hiring cars and driving in Spain *see pages 181–82.*

Coach travel

All the major towns and cities of Andalucía are connected by bus and sometimes by train as well. If you are just hopping between city centres you may as well use them in preference to hiring a car and walk, or take taxis as needs be. See page 182 for full details of coach and rail travel.

Seville has two main bus termini: at Plaza de Armas, near the Puente de Cachorro bridge on the banks of the Guadalquivir, and at Prado de San Sebastián on Avenida de Carlos V, a block away from the Jardines de Murillo. Armas buses head west and north, San Sebastián buses south. Taxi drivers will often ask where you are going and head for the right bus station anyway.

Trains

The Santa Justa rail station has links to Madrid and on to northern Europe, as well as regional destinations such as Cádiz, Córdoba, Granada, Huelva, Málaga and beyond. The RENFE rail network is cheap, clean, (usually) efficient, and can be used to get to most places around Andalucía. It is also the best way to see the country – the Bobadilla–Jimena de la Frontera route is generally regarded as one of the great mountain rail journeys of Europe. There are also some lesser-known services in Andalucía, such as the five-hour high-speed journey from Algeciras to Madrid, or the overnight hotel train to Barcelona that leaves Málaga each evening and arrives the following morning. RENFE has an excellent website with route maps, times and prices, online booking and an English-language edition at *www.renfe.es*

Taxis

Taxi drivers work to a meter and fixed charges for a list of destinations that drivers carry in their cab. There may be an extra charge per item of luggage in the boot. Premium fares kick in late at night and on festival days. Ask for an estimate – *Cuanto cuesta?* (How much?) – if unsure.

Cycling

Cycling as a practical means of travel (as opposed to a sport) is still fairly uncommon in Andalucía, but an awareness of the health and environmental benefits of cycling is growing. The cities have some dedicated cycle lanes, most tourist resorts have bicycle hire facilities and in the countryside there are now *via verdes* (green ways) using abandoned rail tracks as recreational routes. Cycle-touring, however, can be more stressful than rewarding as there are comparatively few minor roads and many are badly signposted. On main roads you should take particular care, as many drivers are completely unaware of the needs of cyclists.

Not all stores take credit cards

Banks and credit cards

Virtually all bank ATMs in Spain are international and will dispense euros against your home account, although not all banks will exchange foreign currency or traveller's cheques. Look for the *Cambio* (change) sign, ideally with a neighbouring *sin comisión* (no commission) notice.

Credit cards (Amex, Diners, VISA, MasterCard etc.) are widely accepted, although not always in smaller shops and restaurants.

Restaurants and bars

The Spanish eat late: lunch is rarely before 2pm, dinner anything between 9pm and midnight or later. Traditionally lunch is the larger meal and dinner a light supper or tapas. Unless a bill stipulates otherwise, service is usually included, although it's considered polite to round up to the tidiest near figure. If you feel you've been well served or the food deserves special thanks, a tip of 10 per cent is sufficient.

Bars vary from tiny hole-in-the-wall kiosks to state-of-the-art designer cocktail joints. Food or a snack is considered an integral part of having a drink with friends, and many bars will serve a free tapa, unasked, with each drink, varied (meat, fish, cheese etc.) depending on the drink. Many will also have a tapas menu with prices. Prices at the bar are often different (cheaper) than table service, and some outdoor bars and restaurants will also charge extra for terrace service. Tipping is discretionary, and less common than in restaurants.

Nightlife

The nocturnal behaviour of the Spanish can baffle even the long-term visitor. Especially in the summer months, they won't think of going out until it already seems late and they can often keep going – usually drinking very little – until well into the morning, or even until it is time to go to work. Few clubs open before 11pm or midnight, most discotheques only really warm up around 2am or later, and most hip nightclubs will tell you not to bother showing up until 4am. Most late-night bars are free, and many nightclubs offer free entry early in the night, with prices (normally covering a first drink) rising as the night proceeds. In some city centre areas, clubs may operate dress codes against jeans and trainers.

Women travellers

While circumstances have changed drastically for women travellers in Spain, certain precautions remain advisable, particularly for the lone traveller. While a younger, educated, generation of males has been learning from its sisters, aunts and female contemporaries, women travelling without men are still considered a cultural anomaly. Women travelling together are sometimes assumed to be lesbian, which might actually work to your advantage. The commonsense precautions for any city or town – avoiding unlit and sparsely populated areas, dressing to avoid snatch thieves, declining unwanted attention politely but firmly, looking as if you know where you're going and so on – apply here as anywhere. Unusually, women travelling with babies or small children can expect the VIP treatment: the Spanish adore children, and hotels and restaurants go out of their way to welcome them.

Gay and lesbian life

The *movida*, movement, of the post-Franco early 1980s triggered an avalanche of social changes, although largely in the cities. Women's rights, lesbian and gay rights and a whole raft of other emancipation movements were swept along by a wave of modernisation that had been held back since the 1960s.

The age of consent for gays and lesbians in Spain is 16, as across the EU. There are large lesbian and gay communities in Cádiz, Granada, Málaga, Seville and the beach resort of Torremolinos. There are often gender-specific bars and cafés, and nightclubs devoted to dress codes such as leather,

Seville's Santa Justa rail station

but most are mixed and often quite popular with heterosexuals as well.

Law

If you happen to encounter, or need the assistance of, Spain's legal system it is best to note that it – or at least its public face – comes armed and isn't terribly friendly.

There are three distinct branches of law enforcement in Spain. The Guardia Civil wear combat-like green militaristic uniforms and have an unfortunate reputation based on their past notoriety as Franco's henchmen. Visitors will probably only encounter them operating spot-checks on motorways. However, in some rural areas, these may be the only law officers on duty.

The Policia Municipal wear a more sedate blue-and-white uniform and are more approachable than the GC. You should seek them or their offices out if you are robbed or mugged, or to report any serious physical or sexual assault. They are more likely to be sympathetic in serious cases and easier to deal with when seeking a crime report, which is essential if you intend to claim stolen property on an insurance policy.

The Policia Nacional in their natty brown riot-response type uniforms are normally only ever seen guarding events of state, controlling crowds and demonstrations, and outside sensitive sites such as embassies, ministry offices and military bases.

Although each of these is armed, the PN heavily so, most visitors to Spain probably won't even notice them. There are some circumstances, however, where forewarned could be forearmed.

Identification: Everyone in Spain, visitors included, is expected to carry some means of identification. All Spanish citizens carry a DNI (National Identity Card). Normally, these are only used to verify ID against credit card transactions. In theory, if you are stopped by the police and don't have ID on you, you can be spot-fined or even arrested and gaoled. Hotels will often keep passports briefly, to confirm identity, but should return them after verification.

Nude or topless bathing: Many resorts have designated nudist bathing beaches, and topless bathing is quite widespread on beaches in more developed resorts. Take local advice and be aware that what might be acceptable dress on the beach can cause offence away from it and in less sophisticated locales. The same applies to dressing to visit churches and other monuments.

Drugs: Spain's drug laws have been in a state of upheaval over the past decade or so. After a period of liberalisation, the signs are that the state's attitude towards drug use is hardening. Despite that, drugs are – perhaps because of Andalucía's proximity to North Africa – quite prevalent in Andalucía, even in small towns, and this includes Class A drugs such as cocaine and Ecstasy and its variants.

Possession of a 'personal use' amount of marijuana (affectionately nicknamed 'chocolate' in Spain) was decriminalised by the Socialist government in 1983. This was later rescinded, although in practice the police have little time or inclination to pursue personal drug use. Things are very different when larger quantities are involved, and the police are likely to be harsher with *extranjeros* (foreigners) found in possession of any quantity of drugs. Spain is under international pressure to render its borders less porous to any forms of smuggling – people, cigarettes and alcohol as much as drugs – and the spread of addiction among even rural communities has hardened people's attitudes to even the less harmful *porro* (joint). In this climate, the visitor should consider dabbling in Spain's drug culture as very much AYOR – at your own risk.

Consulates and embassies

Most countries have consulates or representatives in Seville and Málaga, and embassies in Madrid, who will assist or advise with robberies, loss or theft of passports, emergency repatriation, and so on. If arrested, you have the legal right to contact your consulate, although their willingness to become involved varies from country to country.

Insurance

For Britons and other EU citizens the European Health Insurance Card (EHIC) should smooth access to any necessary medical treatment in accident and emergency or outpatients' departments or at a medical centre. However, the advice to visitors from outside the EU – to take out a travel insurance policy with adequate health and repatriation cover – should also be taken seriously by EU residents. Some treatments and medications can only be obtained privately, and even under a health insurance scheme this will have to be paid for and claimed against the policy.

Seville

Seville leaps out on the unwary first-time visitor. Approached from any direction, by car, bus or train, its skyline starts to bristle with modernist bridgespans, church spires and half-glimpsed monuments such as the Plaza de Toros, the Torre del Oro and, of course, La Giralda tower.

Torre del Oro

The city is a palimpsest of different historical eras and styles, as over the centuries layers of different cultures – Roman, Visigoth, Berber, Almohad, Mudéjar, Gothic, Renaissance, baroque and, across the Rio Guadalquivir, the alarming perspectives and colour-schemes of 20th-century post-modernism around the Expo 92 site – were imposed on each other.

Orientation

The natural place to get your bearings in Seville is in the Plaza del Triunfo. Standing facing the cathedral, with the Giralda tower looming above you, you have the other major sight of Seville, the Reales Alcázares, directly behind you. To your right (eastwards) are the dense streets of Santa Cruz, the most picturesque part of the city.

Parque de María Luisa

Going to your left a few steps takes you past the Archivo de Indias onto the broad Avenida de Constitución. Turn right up this street and cross the square in front of the city hall, and you will reach the main shopping district of the city around Calle de las Sierpes. Keep going in this direction, northwards, and you will be in La Macarena quarter where there are only a few scattered sights to see.

Turning left down Constitución instead takes you towards the Parque de María Luisa and the magnificent Plaza de España. Before you get there you'll pass the university, formerly the tobacco factory of Carmen fame.

Across Avenida de la Constitución from the Plaza del Triunfo, meanwhile, is the old harbourside quarter of El Arenal that stretches down to the banks of the Guadalquivir. Its main sights, the Torre del Oro and bullring, are on the river bank itself. Two bridges lead from here into the Triana district on the other side of the river.

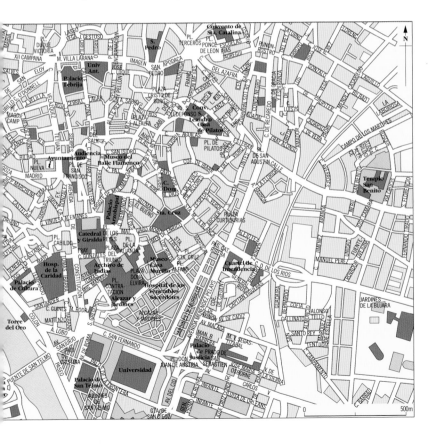

The city

Seville is a remarkably compact city. The city centre consists of four *barrios*, or districts: Santa Cruz, La Macarena, El Arenal and Parque de María Luisa. Most of the key sights are within walking distance of each other: the Giralda tower and cathedral and Reales Alcázares palaces and gardens in Santa Cruz; the Plaza de España and the pavilions of the 1929 Exposition.

Seville's Plaza de España

Lifestyle

The enduring appeal of Seville lies as much in the lifestyle led by its people on its streets as in the grandeur of the historic monuments that loom above them. The mythology insists that, among all the Spanish peoples, the Andalucíans are the most passionate, and the most likely to throw a party.

There is some truth in this stereotype, as can be observed at the annual *Semana Santa* (holy week), leading up to Easter Sunday, when *nazarenos* (penitents) in the pointed hoods and robes of the Inquisition march through the neighbourhoods day and night in a celebration that culminates in an all-night street party. After a short breather of a week or so, the Sevillanos then plunge back into the madness of the *Feria de Abril*, the April Fair, which is the largest in Spain. As the visitor soon discovers, barely a month, or fortnight, passes in Andalucía without some excuse for a party.

A working city

Like other Andalucían cities, Seville lives partly on the direct and indirect revenues derived from tourism, but it is more than a fossilised historical theme park; it is also a working city. As capital of Andalucía it is a politicial, administrative and service centre for southern Spain. It also has a large university that helps stimulate a whole sector of the economy dedicated to culture: concert halls, bookshops, theatres and so on.

Street culture

It is also a city where you will find yourself thrown into the culture as soon as you step outside: unless you hide in your hotel, you will find yourself having breakfast, lunch and dinner elbow-to-elbow with the Sevillanos. Indeed, despite those periods when Atlantic weather systems push up the Guadalquivir valley to drench Seville, much of life is conducted out of doors, even in winter, when the bars of Santa Cruz, Triana and Macarena deploy pavement heaters to warm their patrons. In the outdoor bars around calles Mateos Gago and Rodrigo Caro in Santa Cruz, it is possible to plunge into the street culture of Seville in the shadow of its

Seville

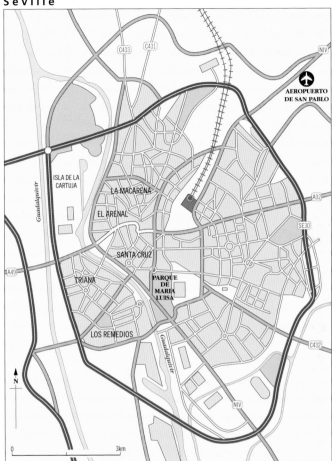

two greatest cultural monuments:
La Giralda tower and the façades of both
the cathedral and the Reales Alcázares.

Exploring Andalucía

Although Seville is an extremely off-
centre capital, situated in the extreme
west of Andalucía, it still forms a good
base for excursions around the region.
It is at the hub of an extremely good

motorway network and there are trains
to all of the other major towns and
cities. Córdoba, Jérez de la Frontera
(famous for sherry) and Doñana
National Park can be visited on day trips
from the city. Granada, Ronda, Málaga
and the white towns of Cádiz are not
much further away: they could be done
in a day each, but are more rewarding
with an overnight stay.

Andalucíans and visitors alike are split over the charms of Seville's Alcázar (fortress) compared to those of its nearest rival, Granada's Alhambra and Generalife gardens. The Alcázar is smaller and more enclosed than the rambling open-air Alhambra, which perhaps gives its courtyards, halls and spectacular décor an intensity lacking in Granada's hilltop monument.

There has been a structure on the site of the Alcázar since Roman times, and palatial accommodation for royalty since the 14th century. It became a fort for the Córdoban caliphate in the 10th century and was expanded by Almohad rulers in the 12th century. Following the reconquest of Seville, King Pedro I, known as Pedro the Cruel to history but Pedro the Just to his cronies, began a programme of expansion that continued sporadically over the centuries.

Patio del León

The Puerta del León, the entrance to the Alcázar, leads through original Almohad walls to the Patio del León courtyard, where Pedro dispensed summary justice after deliberating in the neighbouring **Sala de la Justicia**. Just off the Sala is the exquisite **Patio del Yeso**, a small multi-arched water garden with Almohad designs dating from the 12th century.

Patio de la Monteria

This larger open-air patio, where the court would gather before hunting expeditions, is dominated by the entrance to the Palacio de Pedro I, which gives a hint of the architectural glories to come. The multi-levelled balconied façade is a prime example of the rhythmic patterning of Mudéjar architecture.

Palacio de Pedro I

The upper levels of the Palacio remain the property of the Spanish monarchy even today: King Juan Carlos I has apartments here, where his daughter Elena celebrated her marriage in 1995.

At the heart of the Palacio sits the **Patio de las Doncellas**, the Patio of the Maidens, whose galleried upper floor gives on to a variety of private salons built at various stages in the Palacio's history. Here, in the minutely detailed plasterwork originally fashioned by hand by craftsmen from Granada, the visitor

of *azulejos* (glazed tiling) on the walls. This in turn leads on to the Alcázar's crowning glory, the **Salón de Embajadores**, the 15th-century Ambassadors' Hall, whose stunning domed ceiling, made of interlocking pieces of gilded wood, still dazzles today. It is a masterpiece of design from a culture where representational art was strictly forbidden (*see pp44–5*).

Salones de Carlos V

Things quieten down a little after the Ambassadors' Hall. The Salones de Carlos V were remodelled in the 16th century within an original 13th-century Gothic palace and today house a collection of historic tapestries hung beneath a magnificent vaulted ceiling.

can take a measure of the extraordinary efforts that went into constructing this perfect space intended for the eyes of only a select few. The work that created this perfect symmetry would have taken years.

This effect increases in the neighbouring **Patio de las Muñecas**, the Patio of the Dolls (after two small faces to be found in one of its arches), where the arithmetical repetitions of pattern are enhanced by the strong use

Jardines de la Alcázar

The gardens beyond were originally laid out in the 12th century but are today seen in 16th-century form. The gardens, a symmetrical jungle of towering palms and pines criss-crossed by watercourses and studded with fountains, have to be the most placid spot in the whole of Seville. *Tel: 954 50 23 23; www.patronato-alcazarsevilla.es. Open: Tue–Sat 9.30am–5pm, Sun 9.30am–1.30pm. Admission charge.*

Facing page: Gardens designed for intrigues
Above: Mudéjar arches in the Palacio de Pedro I
Left: The elegant Patio del Yeso at the heart of the Alcázar

Santa Cruz

Catedral entrance

The former Jewish quarter is the liveliest and most historically charged of all Seville's *barrios*. As well as the Reales Alcázares and the cathedral (*see pp36–7*) it also encompasses the Archivo de Indias, the 16th-century repository of documents relating to Spain's conquest of meso-America, the exquisite 17th-century Hospital de los Venerables Sacerdotes, the Jardines de Murillo and the Museo de Arte Contemporáneo.

Of equal interest is the life of this busiest of the *barrios*. Starting on calle Mateos Gagos, leading off the northeast corner of the Plaza del Triunfo, Santa Cruz's scrambled streets and alleys conceal some of Seville's finest bars and restaurants, and not a few of its best hotels as well. Most nights of the week and most weeks of the year, its bars and restaurants are thronged with Sevillanos and visitors who have stumbled on this carelessly kept secret.

Archivo de Indias
At the 'bottom' of the Plaza del Triunfo, this was originally built as a stock exchange to conduct Seville's crucial role as 'office' of the Spanish Americas. In 1785 it was converted into an archive dedicated to collecting documents relating to the colonial enterprise, and is nowadays said to house over 80 million pages of documents, most only available to scholars.
Plaza del Triunfo. Open: Mon–Fri 8.30am–3pm. Free admission.

Callejón del Agua
No visit to Santa Cruz would be complete without a walk along the pedestrianised Callejón del Agua, a narrow alley running beneath the Alcázar garden walls and into the heart of the *barrio*.

Casa de Pilatos
This house was built in the 16th century by the first Marquess of Tarifa as a palatial storeroom for the artworks he gathered on his journeys around Europe and to the Holy Land. Subsequent occupants maintained the tradition and today the Casa rivals the Alcázar in its architectural splendour and the treasures it contains.
Calle Águilas. Open: daily 9am–7pm. Admission charge.

Hospital de los Venerables Sacerdotes
A former retirement home for 'venerable' priests, now used for exhibitions. It has a splendid baroque church.
Plaza de los Venerables. Open: daily 10am–2pm & 4–8pm. Closed: Aug. Guided tours only. Admission charge.

Jardines de Murillo

Plaza Santa Cruz, one of the oldest (1692) and prettiest of the *barrio*'s squares, gives on to these slender public gardens, named after the painter Bartolomé Murillo (1618–82) who lived in nearby calle Santa Teresa, where his former house is now a museum. The gardens feature a towering monument to Columbus.

Gardens open: sunrise–sunset. Museo de Murillo, calle Santa Teresa. Open: Tue–Sun 10am–2pm & 5–9pm. Free.

Museo del Baile Flamenco

A new museum in an 18th-century building, presenting flamenco dance in all its forms from its origins to the present day. There's also a programme of flamenco performances.

Calle Manuel rojas Marcos 3 (near Plaza Alfalfa). Tel: 954 34 03 11; www.museoflamenco.com. Open: 9am–6pm (until 7pm in summer). Admission charge.

Palacio de la Condesa de Lebrija

Around a hundred years ago the passion for all things archaeological, historical and artistic of Doña Regla Manjón Mergelina, Countess of Lebrija, led her to fill her 16th-century ancestral home with any and every object of beauty she could acquire. The result is an eclectic collection housed in an urban mansion, worth seeing in its own right. Many of the pieces – including splendid mosaics – came from the Roman remains at Itálica. Among the other exhibits are Moorish pieces, tiles retrieved from a ruined convent, and a Renaissance frieze.

Calle Cuna 8. Tel: 954 22 78 02; www.palaciodelebrija.com. Open: Mon–Fri 10.30am–1.30pm & 5–8pm, Sat 10am–2pm. Admission charge.

Columbus monument, Jardines de Murillo

Catedral and La Giralda

Seville's cathedral and great bell tower La Giralda sit on the site of a mosque built by Almohad invaders who reached the city in 1147 and set about building the tower and the riverside Torre del Oro. When the Christians took Seville back in 1428, they converted the mosque into a Christian church and began the first of a series of alterations to the tower, starting with its Moorish dome and pinnacle. Today, the Moorish base is capped by a Renaissance belfry housing its fearsome carillon and topped by the Giralda weathervane, the figure of Faith astride the globe.

La Giralda

Catedral

The mosque-church was demolished at the start of the 15th century in favour of a brand new cathedral to accompany the tower. It took over a hundred years to build and when completed was said to be the largest Gothic church in the world. More recent calculations of its floor plan and volume suggest that it may in fact be the largest church in the world.

Capilla Mayor

The most remarkable feature of this church crammed with marvels is the Capilla Mayor, or main altar, dominated by a vast *retablo* (altarpiece) featuring 45 scenes from the life of Christ. As befits the biggest church on the planet, this is also the planet's biggest altarpiece, the life-work of one artist, Pierre Dancart.

Iglesia del Sagrario

This smaller church to the left of the entrance to the nave dates from the 17th century and is nowadays used as a parish church serving the local community.

Patio de los Naranjos

The iglesia opens out into a curiosity in a Christian church: the Patio de los Naranjos, a handsome large courtyard lined with symmetrically planted orange trees. The space dates from the site's period as a mosque, and is where Moorish worshippers would have washed hands and feet in the central fountain before entering the mosque.

Tomb of Columbus

To the right of the vast Capilla Mayor is a small chapel containing the tomb installed in 1890 to house the remains of Columbus, which had been transported here from Cuba. His coffin is supported by four carved figures representing the royal houses of Castille, León, Aragón and Navarra.

Sacristia Mayor

Beyond the tomb, the Sacristia Mayor contains a collection of paintings by Murillo, and a sizeable collection of still more jewelled and gold-bound religious artefacts.

La Giralda

The Giralda tower underwent no fewer than four major changes in design in the first 400 years of its existence, finally reaching the shape we see today in 1568.

The ascent is not as frightening as it looks. La Giralda was built so that two mounted guards could patrol as far up as its belfry. As both men and their mounts needed a shallow gradient, a set of wide and gentle stairs spirals up towards the belfry, which affords magnificent 360-degree views out across the city.
Catedral & Giralda open: Mon–Sat 11am–6pm, Sun 2–7pm. Admission charge. Times may vary: tel: 954 21 49 71 for details.

The giant dome of Seville's Catedral

No one forgets their first encounter with a *nazareno*, one of the hooded and cloaked penitents who form the processions that fill the streets of Seville and every other Spanish city and town during Easter. Accompanied by brass bands and lavishly decorated *pasos* (biers), carrying statues of the Virgin Mary and scenes from the Passion, the figures in their Klan-like disguises can strike terror in the unwitting spectator, and need some explaining.

The marches by local *hermandades* or *cofradias* (brotherhoods) date back as far as the 14th century and the Reconquest. The form they take today dates from the 17th century, when

many of the sumptuous, larger-than-life statues of the Virgin and scenes from Christ's last days (roughly from Gethsemane to Golgotha) were first fashioned. The costumes, which were indeed copied by the USA's Ku Klux Klan for their scare factor, actually come from the anonymous robes of the Spanish Inquisition. At night, lit by braziers, the sight of the *nazarenos* weighed down in their panoply and accompanied by barefoot penitents in chains and rags dragging life-sized crosses behind them, can resemble a tableau from a Gothic horror film. Yet these are largely seen as neighbourhood get-togethers and involve women as well as men, young people and even children. Membership of a *hermandad* is a much sought-after privilege, even by those who wouldn't normally see the inside of a church at any other time of the year.

The routes taken by the *pasos* weave through the streets from each *hermandad*'s local church towards the cathedral, and the further away the church – such as the Basilica de la Macarena – the longer the march: some can be on the streets for 12 hours. The biers can be heavy: depending on their size they can require anything between 40 and 90 bearers, working in relays and swaying in rhythm to displace the weight of the bier. The biers, *nazarenos* and community brass bands are interspersed with groups of local dignitaries and led by a *capataz*, or

captain, who rings a bell to announce regular rest breaks, or sometimes just to let stragglers catch up.

Despite the solemn nature of the marches and the events for which they are atoning, the mood on the pavements is usually celebratory, especially so on Good Friday morning (Thursday from midnight, in fact), which is the climax of the week. (Processions continue until Easter Sunday, although these are less spectacular and thinly attended.) The Thursday daytime processions are sombre affairs, where visitors are asked not to dress in shorts and T-shirts out of respect, but otherwise the atmosphere is one of a long street party. The crowning moment is usually the arrival of La Macarena at the cathedral, usually around 6am on Friday, when even an atheist might feel moved by the Virgin, resplendent in her jewelled gowns and carried aloft on a bier decked with flowers and ablaze with candlelight.

While few other *Semana Santa* celebrations approach the intensity of those in Seville, almost every town and village will have its processions with the statue of the local Virgin Mary and scenes from the Passion. Tourist offices and local newspapers publish timetables and routes for each *hermandad*'s processions through the week.

Facing page and above: *Nazarenos* (hooded and cloaked penitents) in one of Seville's solemn Easter marches

El Arenal

This historic *barrio*, between the Avenida de la Constitución and the Rio Guadalquivir, can claim to be one of the oldest areas of the city. Before the Guadalquivir began to silt up in the 16th century, making it impossible for seagoing craft to reach Seville by the early 17th century, the site of El Arenal was the city's port and the hub of Spain's maritime commerce with the rest of the world.

Plaza de Toros, Seville

Both Columbus and Magellan sailed from here, their sails visible for miles across the flat tidal plains of the Guadalquivir valley. El Arenal's maritime importance stretches further back, however, to the 12th-century Almohad invasion, when the Moors initiated the construction of both the Giralda tower and the Torre del Oro.

Hospital de la Caridad

El Arenal is inadvertently responsible for producing a quasi-mythic figure who himself inspired operas and drama, Don Juan. The 17th-century playboy-turned-philanthropist Miguel de Mañara is wrongly claimed by some to be the model for notorious seducer Don Juan Tenorio. Yet it was Mañara who founded the charitable **Hospital de la Caridad**, still in use today to care for the elderly and infirm. Its chapel contains a small but vibrant collection of paintings by Murillo, Leal and others.
Calle Temprado 3. Open: Mon–Sat 9am–1.30pm & 3.30–7.30pm, Sun 9am–1pm. Admission charge.

Museo de Bellas Artes

This secular masterpiece lies at the northernmost edge of El Arenal. A former convent, the building now houses one of the finest collections of Spanish art under one roof, ranging from medieval to 20th-century but concentrating on the heyday of the 'Seville School' from the 15th century, in particular the works of Murillo, Zurbarán and Leal. The 16th-century convent building, built around three beautiful courtyards and crammed with interior details such as the domed ceiling of its baroque gallery, is worth a visit in itself.
Plaza del Museo. Open: Tue 2.30–8.30pm, Wed–Sat 9am–8.30pm, Sun 9am–2.30pm. Admission charge (EU citizens free).

Plaza de Toros de la Maestranza

Seville's bullring is the oldest and most famous in the world. It was built in 1761 and is not so much a circle as a polygon of 30 sides, with a white and ochre baroque façade facing on to the river

El Arenal and La Giralda seen from Triana

bank. If you can't or don't want to attend a bullfight, you can always take a 20-minute tour of the bullring which takes in not only the arena, but also all the ancillary facilities including the infirmary and chapel.

Paseo de Cristóbal Colón. Tel: 954 22 45 77; www.realmaestranza.com. Open: daily 9.30am–7pm. Admission charge.

Torre del Oro

This tower was originally a watchtower built into the defensive walls that surrounded the Alcázar and the city centre. It was taken back in the Reconquest less than 100 years later, and in the 15th century the tower was used to store bounty brought back from the Americas. Today it houses a modest maritime museum.

Paseo de Cristóbal Colón. Open: Tue–Fri 10am–2pm, Sat–Sun 11am–2pm. Admission charge.

Guadalquivir river cruises

You'll get a different view of the city from the river. **Cruceros Torre del Oro** run one-hour trips every 30 minutes from 10am to 10pm, leaving from the wharf on Alcalde Marqués de Contadero, next to the Torre del Oro. In summer, there are cruises all the way down the river to its mouth at Sanlúcar de Barrameda and Doñana National Park.

For more information, tel: 954 56 16 92; www.crucerostorredeloro.com

Walk: Triana

A walk through the historic *barrio* of Triana across the river from El Arenal is more about capturing the spirit of a place than visiting great monuments – you left those behind as you walked across the Puente de Isabel II (also known as the Puente de Triana). For centuries, Triana was the *gitano* (gypsy) *barrio*, the mythic birthplace of flamenco, and also, coincidentally, the city's pottery district, a craft maintained to this day in its numerous *azulejo* (tiling) workshops.

Allow 2 hours.

1 Capillita del Carmen

The walk begins on the very perimeter of Triana, at the Triana side of the Puente de Isabel II. The curious *azulejo*-clad structure on the right is the Capillita del Carmen, a miniature chapel built in 1926. Directly opposite the Capillita is the distinctive yellow tower of El Faro de Triana, a restaurant whose terraces give great views over the river.

The Puente de Isabel II, or Triana Bridge

2 Calle San Jorge

Take calle San Jorge on the right to plunge into the pottery district, noting particularly the stores on calles Antillano Campos and Covadonga. The most well-known pottery workshop is Ceramica Santa Ana (*San Jorge 31*). *Turning left onto Pages del Corro and then left at San Jacinto, Triana's main thoroughfare, you find calle Rodrigo de Triana on the first right.*

3 Calle Rodrigo de Triana

Named after the sailor who first sighted the New World on Columbus's first trip in 1492, Rodrigo is a typical Triana street, with a view of your next destination, the Iglesia de Santa Ana, above its rooftops.

4 Iglesia de Santa Ana

The dense warren of streets between San Jacinto and the iglesia is where Triana's displaced Roma population lived around communal courtyards, particularly on calle de Pelay Correa.

The church was founded in the 13th century and is said to be the oldest parish church in Seville.

*From the church, walk east towards the river. Either take the calle de la Pureza northwards towards the tiny **Capilla de los Marineros**, the 18th-century sailors' chapel, or continue to the riverfront and walk north along the calle Betis back towards the Puente de Isabel II.*

5 Calle Betis

For many people, calle Betis is the best part of Triana. It can seem like one long line of bars and restaurants pumping out *sevillana* flamenco music. Several of

them have tables set on the river bank, with a few, such as the famous Kiosco de las Flores, in private gardens. All the way there are relaxing views across the water of the bullring and the Torre del Oro, and you can watch canoeists, cruise boats and other river traffic come and go.

You can get back to El Arenal and Santa Cruz the way you came across Puente de Isabel II, but an alternative route is to continue down calle Betis to Plaza de Cuba. From here you can cross the Puente de San Telmo and either turn right into Parque de María Luisa or get back to Santa Cruz via the Puerta de Jerez.

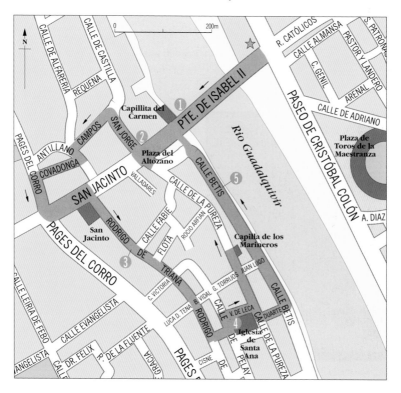

The architecture of other Andalucían cities represents an encyclopaedia of styles imported by invaders across the centuries. Several cultures – Visigoth, Moorish Berber, Almoravid and Almohad – were incorporated into an architecture known as Mudéjar. Later, north European Gothic, Renaissance and baroque flourishes would be added to this mutant form.

Mudéjar itself is a hybrid word, from the Arabic *Mudajjan*, meaning 'those allowed to stay'. This refers both to those Moors who were allowed to convert to Christianity and remain in Spain after the Reconquest, and also to a style of architecture that borrows from previous schools of design.

The classical Moorish arch, as seen in the Mezquita at Córdoba, was taken

from a pattern used in church design by the Visigoths. This was mixed with increasingly elaborate stucco work and the use of religious texts as decorative detail.

Later invaders, such as the Almohads, introduced more formal Islamic styles, such as those seen in La Giralda tower in Seville with its Moorish base and 15th-century Renaissance belfry. The later Nasrid invaders would become responsible for the extraordinary Alhambra and Generalife gardens, while the Mudéjar builders of the Reales Alcázares in Seville borrowed from a variety of designs.

Typically, and bearing in mind the length of time many of these buildings took to complete, or the tendency of later generations to alter, erase or replace earlier structures, some of the larger sites, such as the Alcázar and the Alhambra, represent a mixture of styles. Occasionally these would be used asynchronously, out of the 'order' in which these styles proceeded. A notable example of this is the Mudéjar Palacio de Pedro I, which while Mudéjar in execution is almost entirely Moorish in style – a case, perhaps, of the builders quoting earlier styles to achieve a specific effect.

In almost every era of architecture employed in Moorish Spain, certain features remained constant: air, light, water and space. Running water, rarely very far away in any Moorish or Mudéjar

structure, acted as air conditioning, ionised and cleared air, and aided meditation. Light was mediated through arched galleries and filigree screens such as the Almohad arches of the Patio del Yeso in the Alcázar. Space was kept in proportion but rarely stinted, as the Alhambra, rambling over what is in fact a foothill of the Sierra Nevada mountains, attests.

Two ironies attend the history of Moorish architecture in Spain. While some aspects were assimilated into later styles, the Reconquest set in train a programme of cultural vandalism that saw Moorish masterpieces destroyed or abandoned. Some monuments, such as the Moorish Palacio Mondragón in Ronda, were still languishing in

decrepitude in the latter half of the 20th century.

A greater irony, perhaps, is that where later architectural schools contained homages to or pastiches of earlier styles, it would take an entirely different region of Spain to celebrate Mudéjar and similar styles. While Andalucía abandoned Moorish design to history, late 19th-century Barcelona's *modernistas* (modernists) such as Antoni Gaudí i Cornet and Lluis Domenech i Montaner, adapted Mudéjar – not least its stucco crenellations, rhythmic patterning and use of tiles – for their own dazzling designs.

Beyond the centre

Santa Cruz and El Arenal will certainly be the main claims on your time in Seville, and if you only have a day or two there is no question of where you should spend them. But there are more things to see within a short walking distance to the north into the Macarena district, west to the river and across it, and especially south into the leafy Parque de Maria Luisa. If you prefer to save your legs, hop-on/hop-off tour buses will take you past everywhere worth seeing without you having to leave your seat.

Ceramics in the Plaza de España

Parque de Maria Luisa and the Plaza de España

In 1929 Seville staged the Ibero-American exhibition, a sort of Hispanic world fair that might have been a success if it hadn't taken place in the same year as the Wall Street Crash. However, the city was left with a beautiful park, the Parque de María Luisa, which has a prodigious collection of architecture scattered around it, all of which has been put to good use. Two pavilions, for instance, form museums of archaeology and of folk arts and crafts. The city's finest hotel, the Alfonso XIII, is also a legacy of the exhibition. Even if you are

Icon of La Macarena

not staying there you can go in for a meal or a drink, or simply to escape the noise of traffic for a while.

The most imposing monument in the park is the Plaza de España, a semicircle of arcades ending in two neo-baroque towers. It is decorated with glorious ceramics and has colourful benches depicting the provinces of Spain in alphabetical order.

The Basilica de la Macarena

University (ex-Royal Tobacco Factory)

What is now part of Seville University was once Europe's biggest cigarette factory. It was here that Prosper Merimée's fictional, fiery heroine, Carmen, worked rolling tobacco while she wasn't enflaming men's murderous passions. Bizet took the story and made it the basis of what is perhaps the world's most famous opera.

Basilica de la Macarena

Heading northwards, Santa Cruz merges into the un-gentrified quarter of La Macarena that has several interesting, unvisited churches but is known mostly for the modern. Baroque Basilica de la Macarena, next to some remains of the city's Arab walls, is where the much venerated statue of the Virgen de la Macarena is kept in a position of honour. This 17th-century statuette of the Virgin Mary with tears on her face in grief for her son draws a daily crowd of the faithful who come to make offerings and beg her intercession in their problems. It is ceremoniously brought out of the church by the brotherhood that cares for it during Seville's Easter Week celebrations.

Calle Bécquer 1. Tel: 954 90 18 00; www.hermandaddelamacarena.org. Open: Mon–Fri 9am–2pm, Sat 5–8pm, Sun 9.30am–2pm & 5–9pm. Free admission.

Between April and October 1992, an estimated 36 million people visited the Expo 92 world fair that was held on the Isla de la Cartuja across the Guadalquivir from the centre of Seville. Judged an unqualified success in spite of the expense, Expo turned Seville into a modern city and put it (and Andalucía in general) much higher up the list of must-see destinations than it had previously been. The problem was, and still is, what to do with the Expo site (not an island despite its name) after the last visitor had gone home. Strangely, considering the flagship event that took place there only a few years ago, it is easy to visit Seville and not go near the Cartuja.

But there is charm in exploring what is in effect a post-modern archaeology site. Although many buildings stand empty and crumbling, car parks have become covered by weeds and the once cutting-edge cable car across the river stands forlorn. Several of Expo's innovative pavilions are still there to admire, many of them forming part of a technological business park. Note, however, that Seville's public transport system is as neglectful of the Expo site as the council seems to be, and even if the pavements were in good condition the lack of signposting can make it difficult to find your way around on foot. This might be a good time to sit on the upper deck of a tour bus and have the various pavilions and other Expo leftovers pointed out to you.

Isla Mágica

It's rare to find a theme park in an urban area, but this one around Expo 92's lake is only a short walk across the Puente de la Barquera bridge (a striking bit of architecture in itself) from La Macarena. It means that you don't have to go out of your way to visit it, and can incorporate it into a day of sightseeing. The 40 rides are divided into eight zones.

Tel (information): 902 16 17 16; tel (reservations): 902 16 00 00; www.islamagica.es. Opening times vary greatly throughout the year: check before visiting. Admission charge.

Monasterio de Santa Maria de las Cuevas (Centro Andaluz de Arte Contemporaneo)

If any building could be said to be suffering from schizophrenia, this is it. Built as a Carthusian monastery (after which the Isla de la Cartuja is named) in the 19th century, it was turned into a ceramics factory by a Liverpudlian entrepreneur. In 1992 it briefly served as the centrepiece for Expo, the only old building on the site. Its latest and least interesting incarnation is as a gallery of contemporary art. You can regard the paintings as a bonus, however, as you stroll around the complex admiring the tiled decorations, the patio beside the church and the great ombu tree in the grounds, which is said to have been planted by Christopher Columbus's son, Hernando.

Avenida Amérigo Vespucio 2. Tel: 955 03 70 70; www.caac.es. Open: Tue-Sun. Closed: Mon. Admission charge, but free on Tue. Grounds free all the time.

The entrance to La Cartuja (below), and some of its elaborate tile work (opposite)

Around Seville

It was only natural that, following the conquest of the Americas, Seville's wealth should spill over into the surrounding towns and villages. Seville's eastern flank, towards Córdoba, boasts some of the most beautiful towns in this part of Andalucía.

Carmona's Puerta de Sevilla

Carmona

Its proximity to Seville, combined with a wealth of architectural features and a number of excellent hotels, makes this an ideal alternative to staying in Seville. With a regular (hourly) bus service (*40 mins*) into the centre of Seville, it's also an attractive option for drivers nervous of the capital's streets and reputation for auto crime. At the heart of its warren of medieval streets is a lovely square, the Plaza de San Francisco.

Carmona has been inhabited since pre-Christian Iberian times. Following the Reconquest, it became a country residence for King Pedro I (Pedro the Cruel), architect of parts of the Reales Alcázares and the castle that is now Carmona's *parador*. The Roman presence is preserved today, if only in the fascinating Necrópolis and vestigial auditorium on the outskirts. The town museum and several churches, including San Pedro, with a tower copied from the Giralda, record later architectural and cultural details.

Museo de la Ciudad

Housed in an 18th-century mansion, the town museum has a good collection of artefacts from key eras in the history of the town: prehistoric, Iberian, Roman, Moorish and Christian, including pieces from the Necrópolis.

Calle San Ildefonso. Open: Mon 11am–2pm, Tue–Sun 6–9pm. Admission charge.

Necrópolis Romana

Discovered in 1868, this partially excavated Roman burial site has so far revealed a handful of family tombs, communal crematoria and ossuaries, a villa-like tomb for the daughter of a local ruler and a mausoleum-temple dedicated to the worship of Cybele and Attis. Guided tours (*30 mins*) every 20 minutes.

Avenida Jorge Bónsor. Open: Tue–Fri 9am–5pm, Sat & Sun 10am–2pm. Admission charge, but free to EU citizens.

Écija

Possibly the hottest town in Spain, at the heart of an area known as *la sartenilla* (the frying pan), Écija is an architectural oddity. A total of eleven 15th- and 16th-century church towers dominate its old town centre, a measure, along with its impressive mansions, of Écija's wealth during the Golden Age and its position at the centre of the olive oil industry. The churches and towers are currently in various states of disrepair, and the town's history can be traced in the Museo Historico Municipal.

Museo Historico Municipal, Palacio de Benameyi, Calle Cónovas del Castillo 4. Open: Oct–May Tue–Fri 10am–1.30pm & 4.30–6.30pm, Sat 10am–2pm & 5.30–8pm, Sun 10am–3pm; June–Sept Tue–Fri 10am–2.30pm, Sat 10am–2pm & 8–10pm. Free admission.

Osuna

Built on a small mount in the plains east of Seville, Osuna is another cluster of fine Renaissance mansions topped by a trio of remarkable religious buildings. The lively Plaza Mayor and neighbouring calle San Pedro are the best places to see the (private) mansions, most accessibly the Palacio de los Marquesas de la Gomera, now a five-star hotel.

Clustered above the town are the Colegiata de Santa Maria, the Convento de la Encarnación and the Antigua Universidad.

Situated on the hill above the town. Colegiata and Convento open: Mon–Sat 10am–1.30pm & 4–7pm, Sun 10am–1.30pm. Admission charge.

Osuna's hub, the Plaza Mayor with the town's casino (left) and *Ayuntamiento* – town council – (right)

Jerez de la Frontera

Jerez is the quintessential Andalucían town, the home to *fino* (dry) sherry and to a *gitano* flamenco culture second only to Seville, and the birthplace of classical, horseback bullfighting, still practised today in its bullring. It is also very British, thanks to the presence of sherry dynasties such as Harvey, Williams & Humbert, Domecq, González Byass, Sandeman and others.

Jerez's imposing
Alcázar

There has been a human settlement on the site of Jerez since Phoenician times. The Romans named it Xeres, the Moors Scheris, from which both *jerez* (Spanish for sherry) and sherry derive. The dry white fortified wines produced from the grapes of its temperate vineyards made it the leader of the three key sherry producing towns in Andalucía (*see pp54–5*). The sherry trade also made its sherry dynasties extremely wealthy, a wealth reflected in the monuments and great houses of the town's centre.

Being so close to the great port of Cádiz, it is perhaps unsurprising that Jerez is also a notably industrialised town. The town centre, however, conceals a few architectural delights. It acquired the suffix *de la frontera* (of the frontier) during the Reconquest – probably in the 1390s – when the frontier between Moors and Christians came to rest here.

Centro Andaluz de Flamenco
Jerez sits near the delta of the Rio Guadalquivir valley, which gave Seville and Cádiz their distinctive flamenco cultures. The city's Centro Andaluz de Flamenco is a library, archive, museum and school of flamenco dedicated to keeping the tradition alive beyond the commercialised *tablaos* of the big cities. On most summer season mornings, the centre shows an hourly audio-visual presentation on the history of flamenco. *Plaza de San Juan. Open: Mon–Fri 9am–2pm (Apr–Oct). Free admission.*

The Old Quarter
Numerous monuments jostle for attention in the historic centre. The **Alcázar**, or fortress, is smaller than those in Almería, Málaga and elsewhere but well preserved and boasts a camera obscura offering half-hourly panoramic views over the city. *Alameda Vieja. Open: Mon–Sat 10am–8pm, Sun 10am–3pm. Admission charge.*

Visible downhill from the Alcázar is the town's **Catedral**, whose Gothic basilica was completed in the 18th century. However, the cathedral dates back to the Mudéjar period, notably the free-standing bell tower, and earlier than that to a Moorish mosque originally built on the site. *Plaza de la Encarnación. Open: daily 11am–1pm. Free admission.*

The Gothic cathedral has parts dating back to before the Reconquest

Real Escuela Andaluz de Arte Ecuestre

Jerez's annual May Feria del Caballo (horse fair) is the biggest country fair in the entire Andalucían calendar. Outside the *feria*, the city's famous Real Escuela Andaluz de Arte Ecuestre is Andalucía's premier school for training horses and their riders. On some mornings you can observe dressage practice and every Thursday morning in season the school also stages a full performance in which horses and riders are accompanied by classical music.

Avenida Duque de Abrantes. Open: Mon, Wed & Fri 11am–2pm, except Aug. Admission charge. Full performance Tue & Thur at noon. Admission charge.

Sherry Bodegas

The Alcázar overlooks two of Jerez's most famous bodegas, Domecq and González Byass. They and the Harvey,

Sandeman, Wisdom & Warter and Williams & Humbert bodegas (all within walking distance) offer tours and tastings (mostly mornings). Booking is not necessary, but advisable if you are on a tight schedule.

González Byass, calle Manuel González. Tel: 956 35 70 00. Tours daily at 11.30am, 12.30pm, 1.30pm, 2pm, 3.30pm, 4.30pm & 5.30pm. Admission charge.

Domecq, calle San Ildefonso. Tel: 956 15 15 00. Tours Mon–Fri at 10am, 11am, noon & 1pm, Sat noon & 2pm. Admission charge.

Sandeman, calle Pizarro. Tel: 956 15 17 00. Tours Mon, Wed & Fri 11am, noon, 1pm & 2.30pm. Admission charge.

Williams & Humbert, calle Nuño de Cañas. Tel: 956 35 34 06. Open: Mon–Fri 9am–3pm. Admission charge.

Harveys, Pintor Muñoz Cebrión. Tel: 956 15 15 00. Tours Mon–Fri 10am & noon. Admission charge.

The Sherry Triangle

Wine and, in particular, sherry has been produced in western Andalucía for at least 3,000 years, having been introduced by Phoenician traders. Under Greek and Roman invaders, the Jerez region became a centre for sherry production and export throughout the Mediterranean. The teetotal Moors were largely indifferent to its alcoholic qualities, although their medicinal alembic, or still, would later find non-medical uses in distilleries around the globe.

British wine traders arrived in the pacified Spain following the Reconquest and set about carving up the sherry trade. The region's dry, chalky soil, temperate mix of sunshine and Atlantic weather systems, and, most importantly of all, the *solera* (vintage, or tradition) production process made it perfect for producing sweet (*oloroso*) and dry (*fino*) sherries. Three towns or areas make up the so-called Sherry Triangle: Sanlúcar de Barrameda, Jerez and the area around Cádiz and El Puerto de Santa Maria.

There are five main types of sherry, including the *oloroso* and *fino*. The latter, typified by brands such as Domecq's La Ina, is by far the more popular in bars and as an aperitif, usually drunk chilled from the fridge. *Amontillado* is a stronger form of *fino*, one in which the *flor* (yeast) has been allowed to develop a richer, sometimes dry, sometimes sweet, taste. Cream, most famously as bottled as Harvey's Bristol Cream, is a blend of *oloroso* and sun-dried Ximénez grapes.

Sherry production follows that of wine, with two crucial later stages. During fortification, distilled grape spirit is added, which increases alcohol content to 18 per cent for sweet and 15 per cent for dry. The sherry is stored for three months in wooden barrels where young sherry is gradually filtered down through a succession of barrels

containing older sherry. The final mix of old and young is then bottled. Other random processes – the quality of harvest, the appearance of *flor*, and the drying of grapes for Pedro Ximénez dessert sherry – also produce variations on the *oloroso/fino* process.

Manzanilla, produced exclusively in the handsome sea town of Sanlúcar de Barrameda on the mouth of the Guadalquivir, is considered an entirely different type of sherry. Aficionados insist that its light, drier taste is far superior to *fino*. *Manzanilla* is unfortified, and romantic myth claims that its special flavour comes from salty sea breezes blowing in across the vineyards. A more likely explanation would be soil, irrigation and climate. Just as in Jerez, Sanlúcar's *manzanilla* bodegas, such as La Guita, offer guided tours and tastings.

The third point of the Sherry Triangle is the area around Cádiz and neighbouring El Puerto de Santa María (a fast-developing tourist alternative

to Cádiz itself, and served by a swift ferry service), which both produce *fino* from vineyards in the surrounding Guadalquivir valley.

Fino and *manzanilla* are the Andalucían tipple of choice for socialising. One of the best ways to sample *manzanilla* is at the huge tapas festival that takes place on Sanlúcar's central boulevard, Alzado de Ejercito, in the second week of October. The Andalucían passion for *jerez* reaches its peak during the fiestas such as the *ferias* that take place in the different cities over the summer, which are staggered at different dates through the month: townsfolk hang *copitas* (small glasses in leather holsters) around their necks and share bottles among themselves as they carouse in the streets.

Facing page: Sherry is stored for three months in wooden barrels
Above: Jerez is home to many sherry dynasties, including González Byass

Cádiz

Said to be the oldest city in Europe, Cádiz has character, history, culture and lifestyle to give Seville a run for its money. Once notorious as a sleazy port full of rough bars and bordellos, it has tidied up its act over the decades while retaining the tang of its racier times. Isolated on a slender promontory jutting into the Atlantic, it is renowned for its Carnaval (in February or March).

Plaza de España

The old town of Cádiz, north of the monumental Puertas de Tierra gates, is a maze of weather-worn mansions and monuments. A narrow street, variously named as it winds around the town, circles the seafront, and connects, for example, the RENFE station on Plaza Sevilla, the Bahia de Cádiz beach, the exquisite Parque Genovése topiary gardens and the modern *parador*, the Playa de la Caleta and the Plaza de la Catedral. The city centre between these can be traversed in a matter of minutes.

As well as its historic Carnaval, Cádiz has a very lively university culture supporting music venues, clubs, book and music stores, and a high-profile gay community who are the life and soul of Carnaval and just about any other excuse to party. It also goes without saying that Cádiz is a fish-eater's paradise: only a fool would leave Cádiz without sampling either the restaurant or tapas bar at its legendary El Faro (*calle San Felix 15*).

Catedral Nuevo

Cádiz's cathedral, called the 'new' cathedral because it sits on the site of an earlier church, is a mountainous baroque and neoclassical edifice looming magnificently over the Plaza de la Catedral. Its bright yellow-orange tiled cupola and neoclassical towers act as a guidance beacon wherever you walk across town. Although of minor historic detail, it is noted as the last resting place of probably the most famous *gaditano*, as the people of Cádiz are known, composer Manuel de Falla (1876–1946).

The monumental Puertas de Tierra gates

Plaza de la Catedral. Open: Tue–Fri 10am–1.30pm & 4.30–8.30pm, Sat 10am–1pm. Admission charge.

Museo de Cádiz

Near the cathedral, the museum dedicated to the history and culture of Cádiz tracks the city's development from prehistoric times to the present day. On its second floor is a sizeable art gallery, dedicated to works by Murillo, Rubens and Zurburán.

Plaza de Mina. Open: Tue 2.30–8.30pm, Wed–Sat 9am–8.30pm, Sun 9.30am–2.30pm. Admission charge, but free for EU citizens.

The Catedral Nuevo from the seafront

Museo de las Cortes de Cádiz

The history of this famously liberal city is celebrated in the city museum, which displays many of the papers relating to the short-lived independent government of the 1810s. Its neighbouring **Oratorio de San Felipe Neri** is the place where the Cortes sat and is also open to the public. *Calle Sante Inés. Museo open: Tue–Fri 9am–1pm & 4–7pm. Sat 9am–1pm. Free. Oratorio open: Mon–Sat 10am–1pm. Admission charge.*

Plaza de España

Much of historic Cádiz is centred around the Plaza de España, which is dominated by the **Monumento a las Cortes Liberales**, the monument to Spain's first liberal government, established briefly in Cádiz in the 1810s before being quashed by the monarchy.

Torre Tavira

This 18th-century watchtower in the heights above the city is just one of the numerous military installations that offer views back over Cádiz. It features a camera obscura with a 360-degree panorama of the city. *Calle Marqués de Real Tesoro. Open: daily 10am–6pm (until 8pm mid-June–mid-Sept). Admission charge.*

Walk: Cádiz

Cádiz is the perfect walking city, a maze of 18th-century streets and squares crammed into the tip of a slender promontory jutting into the Atlantic. With most new-build projects – the motel-like *parador* excepted – barred from the old quarters, it is also the most atmospheric of all the *cascos antiguos* (old quarters) of Andalucía.

Allow 3 hours.

1 Puertas de Tierra

These monumental walls were part of the city's 18th-century defences when Andalucía's world trade centre moved to Cádiz from Seville following the silting of the Rio Guadalquivir.

2 Carcel Vieja

This walk heads west into the afternoon sun along Concepción Arenal and past the Carcel Vieja, or old prison, towards the cathedral.

Playa de la Caleta, Cádiz's most popular beach

3 Catedral Nuevo

The cathedral looms over the Plaza de Pio XII, also known as the Plaza de la Catedral. Cathedral and square give off a weird oceanic light like a glow from the sea just behind it.

Follow the sea road on towards the Castillo de San Sebastian fortifications (not open to the public).

4 Playa de la Caleta

The fortifications overlook one of Cádiz's most popular beaches, the Playa de la Caleta. *Continue along the sea road to the Castillo de Santa Catalina.*

5 Castillo de Santa Catalina

At the north end of the bay, matching the Sebastian sea defences across the bay, sits the citadel of Santa Catalina, built in 1598.

Open: daily 10.30am–6pm. Free admission.

6 Parque del Genovése

From the Castillo, these exquisitely sculpted topiary walkways look like a backdrop out of a de Chirico painting. *Turn right at the southern end of the park along calle Benito Pérez Galdos.*

7 Calle Benito Pérez Galdos

The calle heads into the heart of the town to the Gran Teatro Falla and its plaza. Continue straight on to the Oratorio de San Felipe Neri and the Museo Histórico Municipal, site of and archive to the historic 1812 constitution. *From here you can either retrace your steps to follow the sea road or head a few blocks north via calle Sagasta to the Plazas de San Francisco and de Mina.*

8 Museo de Cádiz

Comprising the Museo de Bellas Artes and the Museo Arqueológico, the museum has Phoenician and Roman displays on its ground floor, a fine arts collection including works by Rubens, Zurburán and Murillo on the second and an ethnology department.

9 Plaza de España

A few blocks east of Plaza de Mina is the Plaza de España. Beyond it lies the seafront of the Puerto Commercial; northwards, steps lead up on to modern-day defences with views over the town. *The Avenida del Puerto runs eastwards to the Paseo de Canalejas and the Plaza de San Juan de Dios.*

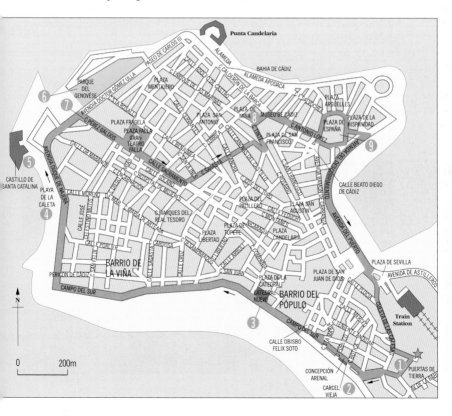

Wherever you go in Andalucía in the week running up to Lent, you will find communities large and small celebrating Carnaval, although none of them with the vigour of Cádiz. Carnaval was originally the last chance to unwind before the forty days of austerity, although few people nowadays observe Lent.

Community and religious groups, professional and youth organisations, and groups of friends roam the streets (usually in the evening and late at night) entertaining crowds, bars and restaurants with pithy and sometimes rude or libellous satirical songs on events of the day. Most groups will enter competitions judged in the town theatre, such as Cádiz's Teatro Falla, while others just take to the streets for the hell of it. Others seize the opportunity to run amok in drag, fancy dress, or as *gigantes*, blobby monsters wielding balloons on sticks on a mission to hunt down every child and tourist and wallop them over the head.

The idea, as perhaps is already apparent, is to have as much good-natured fun as is possible this side of getting arrested. And compared to similar events elsewhere in Europe, Andalucía's Carnavales are remarkably good-natured and convivial affairs. Each climaxes in a *cabalgata*, or cavalcade,

where, however modest the display, children of every conceivable age find themselves engulfed in blizzards of confetti and confectionery hurled by retinues of the town's beauty queens from their gaudily decorated floats.

The notoriety of Cádiz's Carnaval, which stems from both its rumbustious seaport culture and its healthy tradition of resistance to state control, is given further resonance by the fact that it was the only Carnaval that Franco was too scared to ban, fearing that a ban might spark insurrection. It is very much a celebration in the hands of the people, and one where the revellers in this most poverty-stricken region of Spain have over the centuries found at least symbolic ways to wreak revenge on bosses, politicians and the hated *caciques* (foremen) of the despised *latifundistas*.

Even on the storm-prone Atlantic coast, February can be kind and sunny during daytimes, although evenings can be distinctly chilly. Most revellers seem to survive on piping hot food, alcohol, aerobic motion among the crowds in the streets and generously layered undergarments.

Anyone hoping to join the celebrations in Cádiz itself, and to a lesser degree in Seville and Granada, should begin planning and making accommodation enquiries the preceding autumn – Cádiz's hotels can fill up months ahead for Carnaval. Alternatives include staying in the burgeoning resort of Puerto de Santa María across the Bahia de Cádiz, with ferry connections to Cádiz's old town during daytimes, or further afield in Jerez or Seville. Late night and early morning trains to both are often full of revellers returning home from Cádiz, and both cities will also be celebrating their own Carnavales. Any of the larger cities will provide a launchpad to smaller, local Carnavales, with tourist offices able to supply key days and venues, and which, while modest, offer a glimpse into *la vida Andaluz* unseen by the summer visitor.

Andalucía's Carnavales are good-natured and convivial affairs

Costa de la Luz

Spain's little-visited Atlantic Costa de la Luz – 'coast of light' – is one of the best-kept secrets in Europe. Although the great Rio Guadalquivir estuary and a number of ports interrupt it, its 200km (125-mile) beach is the longest – and cleanest – in Spain, perhaps the whole of southern Europe. Its climate is also kinder than you might expect from an Atlantic coastline.

Tarifa beach

Stretching from medieval Tarifa (*see pp70–71*) to Isla Cristina near the Portuguese border, the costa passes two of Spain's greatest seaports, the largest bird and nature reserve in Europe, Roman ruins, various grand seaside towns and the most unspoilt beaches in the whole of Spain.

History

As the handsome Roman ruins of Bolonia (*see p69*) north of Tarifa's world-class surf beaches (*see pp70–71*) attest, explorers had rounded the Pillars of Hercules to explore Atlantic Spain as early as the second century BC. Bolonia became famous throughout the Empire for a spicy fish paste, garum, used as a relish by the wealthier classes.

Even earlier settlers such as the Phoenicians had already brought viniculture to the region, at Cádiz and elsewhere, and fishing ports at Zahara de los Atunes and its (rather scruffy) neighbour, Barbate. The latter does, however, have one major claim to fame: nearby Cabo de Trafalgar overlooked the 1805 battle which saw England's fleet under Nelson defeat the French and

Spanish, although at some personal cost to the admiral.

Coast of Cádiz

The main reason that the Costa de la Luz is one of Europe's best-kept secrets is that holidaymakers from Seville, Cádiz, Huelva and elsewhere tend to keep resorts such as **Conil** and **Chiclana** to themselves. Both are classic bucket-and-spade resorts, with little else to commend them, although Conil has a photogenic town square and medieval tower with connections to the legend of Guzman the Good, defender of Tarifa (*see pp70–71*).

The coast of light vanishes beneath the salty lagoons of Cádiz to re-emerge at the garish resort of **Rota**, a favourite for US servicefolk on R&R, and the golden strands of **Chipiona**. However, given the proximity of **Sanlúcar de Barrameda**, you should push on to this atmospheric town with its mansions, *manzanilla* bodegas and fine beaches.

Huelva province

Huelva is the westernmost and least interesting of the eight Andalucían provinces. Its short coast from **Matalascañas** (at the northern limit of Doñana National Park) to the Portuguese border has some fine deserted beaches backed by sand dunes, punctuated by only two or three resorts – **Mazagón**, **Puerta de Umbria** and **Isla Cristina**. The city of **Huelva** itself is utterly missable, but makes a useful base from which to explore the Columbus sites nearby. Inland Huelva, however, has some attractive countryside, particularly in the **Sierra de Aracena**. Huelva's most famous town, **El Rocio**, is a nondescript place if visited at any time of year other than Whitsun, when it is the objective of Andalucía's famous mass pilgrimage (*see page 21*).

One of the best beaches on the entire Costa de la Luz, below Valdevaqueros dune system

History may have changed its attitude towards 15th-century explorer Christopher Columbus recently, but he remains very much a hero in western Andalucía. He sailed from Palos de la Frontera (near Huelva), Seville, Cádiz and Sanlúcar de Barrameda on his four voyages to the Americas, and is celebrated in statuary and other monuments throughout the region.

Born in Genoa, Italy, in 1451, Cristóbal Colón, as he is more commonly known in Spain, gained his reputation as an adventurer in the Mediterranean and Iberian Atlantic before deciding to search for the fabled westerly route to the Orient. Portugal rebuffed his proposal, but the Spanish monarchs Isabel and Fernando (the former especially) agreed to fund his expedition.

Columbus returned from one of his four expeditions to the Americas a criminal in chains, following his disastrous mismanagement of an uprising, and his treatment of indigenous Americans was appalling, if par for the era. Yet his piracy and plunder funded Spain's Golden Age, and sketched out a map of geopolitics still discernible today.

La Rábida

This monastery at the mouth of the Rio Tinto estuary south of Huelva is the main Columbus site in Andalucía. He visited the monastery while pursuing support for his expedition, debating with its theologians and seeking divine guidance for his schemes. Today, the monastery is part of a larger theme-park-like enclosure, with gardens,

exhibits, and replicas of the caravelles *Santa María*, *Nina* and *Pinta* with which he sailed on his first voyage in 1492.

Guided tours of the monastery run almost hourly each day, taking in his living quarters, murals of the expeditions and the chapel where fellow explorer Martín Alonso Pinzón, captain of the *Pinta*, is interred.

The replicas of Columbus's three ships are moored at the **Muelle de las Carabelas** (caravel pier), where there is also an exhibit dedicated to his life and exploits.

Monasterio de La Rábida: 8 km (5 miles) south of Huelva on N-442. Tel: 959 35 04 11. Open: Tue–Sun 10am–1pm & 4–6pm (hourly tours). Closed: Mon. Admission charge. Muelle de las Carabelas open: Tue–Fri 10am–2pm & 5–9pm, Sat–Sun 11am–8pm. Closed: Mon. Admission charge.

Palos de la Frontera

This small village a short journey inland from La Rábida is the port from which Columbus and his crew left in 1492. The captains of the *Pinta* and *Nina*, cousins Martín and Vicénte Yañez Pinzón, came from here, and they and their crews are celebrated

in a monument outside the beautiful town **church**, where Columbus and his men celebrated communion on the eve of departure, and in the **Museo Martín Alonso Pinzón** in the town centre.

Museo Martín Alonso Pinzón, calle Cristóbal Colón 24. Open: Mon–Fri 10am–1pm & 5–7pm. Free admission.

Moguer

This immensely atmospheric, if slightly crumbly, town further inland on the Rio Tinto is where many of the three ships' crews came from. The most noteworthy connection with the Columbus legend is the **Monasterio de Santa Clara**, where Colón honoured a promise, made when he was spared a storm that nearly wrecked the enterprise off the Azores, to keep a vigil for a night on his return from the 1492 voyage.

Monasterio de Santa Clara, calle Monjas. Open: guided visits Tue–Sat 11am–1pm & 5–7pm. Closed: Mon & holidays. Free admission.

Facing page: Replica boats at La Rábida, near Huelva
Above: The Columbus statue at La Rábida

Doñana National Park

The largest nature reserve in Spain and one of the largest in Europe, Doñana stretches from Sanlúcar's further shore halfway to Seville, north as far as El Rocio and halfway up to Huelva along the Costa de la Luz (*see pp62–3*). As well as its indigenous wildlife, it is also a stopping-off point for an estimated six million migratory birds on their biannual routes north and south in spring and autumn.

Parkland walkway

Terrain

The Parque Nacional de Doñana was declared a protected area in 1969 for fear that encroaching farming and development might threaten this unique wetland environment. Scientists in fact describe the region as man-made, as over the centuries farming, fishing, hunting and other activities have subtly and not-so-subtly altered its shape and the flora and fauna it supports. The park comprises the *marismas* (marshes) of the rios Guadalquivir and Guadiamar, the former here debouching into the Atlantic after its journey from its source 700km (435 miles) away in the Sierra de Cazorla in northwest Andalucía.

Wildlife

As well as its migratory visitors, which in winter months include vast flocks of flamingos feasting on shrimp, the park is also home to fallow and red deer, lynx, boar, mongoose and several rare raptors, including the imperial eagle.

Visiting the park

Visitor numbers in Doñana are strictly limited. If you are just mildly curious or have little time, the best way to get to know a little about the park is to go to one of the five visitors' centres on the edges of the restricted area. The one at Aznalcázar (*open: 10.30am–7pm*) is closest to Seville but the best one for an introduction to Doñana's wildlife is Acebuche (*open: 8am–9pm*) reached via El Rocío, a town famous for its Whitsuntide pilgrimage.

The only way to appreciate Doñana fully is to devote time to it and take a guided tour in a 4×4 vehicle. This takes 4 hours and ranges over 70km (43 miles), sampling a little of all the ecosystems that make up the park.

An alternative way to visit Doñana is to take a boat trip from the Fabrica de Hielo visitors' centre located at Bajo de Guía (on the outskirts of Sanlúcar de Barrameda). Of course, the wildlife you do or do not see depends on the time of year and luck. Mammals are particularly difficult to see but birds are more visible especially during the spring and autumn migrations.

Guided 4×4 tours Trips leave from Acebuche visitors' centre. *Tel: 959 43 04 32. Tours depart: June–mid-Sept*

Only a few hundred visitors a day are allowed into the 81,000ha (200,000 acre) nature reserve

Mon–Sat 8.30am & 5pm; mid-Sept–May Tue–Sun 8.30am & 3pm. Booking essential.
Boat trips *Tel: 956 36 38 13;*

www.visitasdonana.com. Departures from Bajo de Guía: Nov–Feb 10am; Mar–May & Oct 10am & 4pm; June–Sept 10am & 5pm. Reservations essential.

Andalucía occupied a position of great privilege in the western Roman Empire for 500 years from the 2nd century BC to the 3rd century AD. Following centuries of rule by Carthage, the great Mediterranean force in what is nowadays Tunisia, the inhabitants of the southwestern tip of the peninsula welcomed the Roman invaders, and certainly thrived on the culture they introduced. Roman Baetica, as the region was known, was almost identical in outline to modern-day Andalucía.

Carthage was already on the wane when the Romans invaded this part of the peninsula in the last decade of the 3rd century BC. They began construction of their greatest settlement, Italica, just north of Seville, in 206 BC. The thriving seaport at modern-day Bolonia, Baelo Claudia (named after the emperor

Claudius) followed. So, in the 1st century AD, did Acinipo, the extensive ruined settlement on a windswept bluff outside Ronda, as Ronda la Vieja, 'old Ronda'.

Italica

At its height, around the 1st century AD, Italica was one of the greatest cities in the Roman Empire, a rival to even Alexandria and Rome. Its population reached half a million, and its monumental amphitheatre, visible in part today, held in excess of 25,000 people. The Visigoths simply abandoned the site for their preferred base of Seville, while later rulers plundered the site for materials (including the stone columns that now surround Seville Cathedral).

Also still visible are the vestiges of several halls and mosaics, foundations and men's and women's baths.

Santiponce. 5km (3 miles) north of Seville. Open: Tue–Sat 9am–8pm, Sun 10am–4pm. Admission charge (EU citizens free).

Baelo Claudia

This smaller but less vandalised site sits on the beach at Bolonia north of Tarifa. Although less impressive than Italica it includes the remains of a forum, baths, an open-air auditorium, temples to Juno, Jupiter and Minerva, and other religious buildings. Near the beach is the vestigial fish factory responsible for garum, an alarming paste of fish parts that was shipped throughout the Empire and revered as the best caviar is today.

Baelo Claudia, Bolonia beach. 15km (9 miles) north of Tarifa on N-340. Open: June–Sept Tue–Sat 10am–8pm; rest of the year 10am–6pm, Sun 10am–2pm. Admission charge.

Acinipo/Ronda la Vieja

Known by either of these names on local maps and road signs, this has one of the most spectacular settings in the whole of Andalucía: it lies on a slope rising to one of a series of bluffs above rolling farmland east of Ronda, with views of the sierras to the north.

A dig in progress like Baelo Claudia, Acinipo has so far yielded a magnificent open-air theatre and auditorium, the groundworks of a triple hot water baths, fragments of a forum, a skeletal street grid and piles of what were once the rock walls of the town itself. Its remote site left it prone to ransackers over the centuries.

Acinipo, on MA-499 Ronda–Setenil. Open: Tue–Sun 9am–3pm. Free admission.

Facing page above: The windswept Roman ruins of Ronda la Vieja, 'old Ronda'
Facing page below: Vestigial remains at Bolonia
Below: Backstage at the monumental theatre in Roman Acinipo

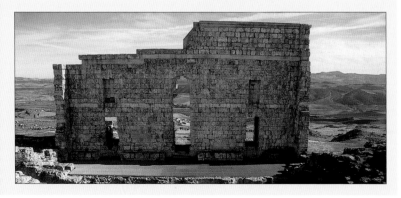

Tarifa's Mudéjar Puerta de Jerez

Tarifa and the Surf Coast

In recent years Tarifa has been declared the most fashionable medieval city in Spain, possibly one of the most fashionable in the whole of Europe. An accident of local winds and tides, an embarrassment of glorious sandy beaches and the efforts of the surfie grapevine have elected it one of the three great surf destinations in the world.

The town is named after its 8th-century invader, Tarif ben Maluk, who made a successful sortie to the European mainland to scout the land for Tariq ibn Ziyad's invasion of Gibraltar in AD 711. While its medieval walls and street plan remain, it has changed rather drastically over the past decade. Every other storefront in its maze-like walled Moorish old town is a boutique, gear store, cybercafé or bar dedicated to the shrimpcatcher-shorts set. Traditionally a laid-back hideaway, popular with backpackers on their way to and from North Africa, its new-age emporia now find themselves serving a new generation of beach bums.

Tarifa is also, unsurprisingly, a party town, nowhere more so than in the bars, cafés and restaurants around calle Sancho IV in the centre. It is also worth pointing out that while some of its best hotels, such as the Amarillo and la Sacristia, are here, most visitors head for the beach hotels such as the Hurricane and Dos Mares a dozen or so kilometres north.

Tarifa's beaches themselves begin unprepossessingly but improve around the Hurricane hotel and are at their best by the dune systems of Valdevaqueros,

where hardcore surfers can be found at play year-round.

Castillo de Guzmán

Parts of the handsome ramparts are still used by the Spanish naval authorities and off-limits to visitors, but Tarifa's most imposing structure, the Castillo de Guzmán, is currently undergoing restoration and will be reopened to the public. Built on the site of a 10th-century Moorish *alcázar*, itself built on the site of a Roman fort, this was rebuilt as a *Reconquista* castle in the 11th century. The castle acquired its name and its place in history during the 1292 Moorish siege of Tarifa, when the Christians defended the town against invaders from Morocco. Its name derives from the honorific title awarded by the people to Alonso Pérez Guzmán, Guzmán el Bueno (Guzmán the Good), the castle's commander, who sacrificed his son, who had been taken hostage by the invaders rather than surrender the town. *Closed for restoration.*

Iglesia de San Mateo

Also of interest is the Iglesia de San Mateo, on the corner of calles Moscardo

and Copons, begun in the 15th century but only completed in the 18th. The dilapidated baroque exterior conceals a surprisingly modern interior.
Open: daily 9am–1pm & 5.30–8.30pm. Free admission.

Museo Municipal
Near the castle, on the picturesque Plaza de Santa María, are the *ayuntamiento* and the small Museo Municipal, with a modest but respectable collection of neolithic, Roman and Moorish artefacts.
Museo Municipal, Plaza de Santa María. Open: daily 11am–1pm. Free admission.

Whale watching
As well as surfie boutiques, Tarifa has more than its fair share of emporia offering dolphin- and whale-watching expeditions. The most ecologically sound thing to do would be to leave these beautiful creatures in peace, but if you have to see them it's best to go with non-profit-making organisations such as Whale Watch (*Avenida de la Constitución 6; tel: 956 62 70 13*) or the Foundation for Information and Research on Marine Mammals (*calle Pedro Cortés; tel: 956 62 70 08*).

Kite surfing, mixing parachuting with windsurfing, at Tarifa beach

Gibraltar

Officially British, geographically part of Andalucía, and ethnically a mix of all the races that have ever passed through, this small territory of disputed sovereignty is an anomaly in almost every sense, and for that it has its undeniable attractions. There is a quaint faux Britishness to the place, even if most of the English you hear will be delivered in an Andaluz accent.

Gibraltar's Rock

A stroll along Gibraltar's central Main Street from Casemates Square to beyond the cathedral, with its preponderance of duty-free stores, fast food outlets and British pubs, might have you assuming that this is nothing more than a

Main Street, Gibraltar's liveliest thoroughfare

shopping centre. Old Gibraltar hands, however, point out that there is another Gibraltar away from this shopping mall-cum-virtual casino, in its handsome old back streets and squares.

Visiting Gibraltar

As the odd disappointed shopper or baffled taxi driver discovers, you need a passport to pass between Spain and Gibraltar. Visitors from EU countries, the USA, Canada, Israel and South Africa do not require visas: visitors from elsewhere should check the current state of visa requirements before visiting what is still a sensitive military base – Gibraltar still has an active British military presence.

Gibraltar trades in Gibraltarian sterling, not negotiable elsewhere, or the euro.

Getting there and around

Drivers are advised to park in Spain and walk across the border: delays are frequent and access is cut off whenever a flight lands on the runway of the small but busy airport between the border and the centre.

There are local and regional bus connections with La Linea de la Concepción, the town on the Spanish side of the border crossing, and bus or taxi links between the rail stations at either San Roque/La Linea or Algeciras.

The Rock
Inevitably, the Rock of Gibraltar is the most interesting part of the colony to visit. Unless you like hill walking, the best policy is to take the cable car up and walk down. From the top station (which incorporates a restaurant) there are fabulous views over the town and harbour of Gibraltar, of Algeciras in Spain and, on a clear day, of the North African coast.

Cute but dangerous: the Rock's macaque monkeys are notorious bag snatchers and can bite

Much of the Rock is a nature reserve protected for its flora that includes two indigenous plants. And, of course, the Rock is inhabited by Barbary apes – in fact a species of tailless monkey introduced by the British in the 18th century. These curious and mischievous creatures can snatch cameras and handbags and react aggressively when they feel threatened. Keep your distance, keep calm and they won't bother you.

From the cable car top station, paths zigzag back down into town. Some 50km (31 miles) of tunnels have been carved into the Rock for military reasons and some sections are open to the public, such as the Great Siege Tunnels that were dug by the British Army in 1779–83. They're only really worth visiting, though, if you are interested in military history.

What to see
Gibraltar Museum
Halfway along Main Street, to the right beyond the Cathedral of St Mary the Crowned, is the Gibraltar Museum. Its small but impressive display of artefacts ranges from the Moorish invasion of the Iberian peninsula up to its maritime exploits in recent centuries.
Gibraltar Museum, Bomb House Lane. Open: Mon–Fri 10am–6pm, Sat 10am–2pm. Admission charge.

Ronda

Few towns have a setting as dramatic as Ronda, the most famous of the so-called White Towns (Pueblos Blancos) of Andalucía. Not only does it nudge up to a vertiginous cliff, but it also straddles a deep gorge. For its setting alone, Ronda is a magnet for coach parties coming up from the Costa del Sol. Fortunately it hasn't quite turned itself into a cliché, although it could easily do so as it promotes itself these days as the cradle of modern bullfighting and the former haunt of *bandoleros*.

Ronda's Puente Nuevo bridge

Ronda has good road and rail links with Seville and Málaga, and a large choice of hotels and restaurants. As such it makes an excellent base for exploring the other white towns that dot the surrounding sierras.

Puente Nuevo
Almost every view of Ronda shows the 98-m (321-ft) high 'new bridge' striding across the Tajo gorge. It was built in 1793 and is called the 'new' bridge because an earlier attempt to span the gap ended fruitlessly with the deaths of 50 people. The bridge has a visitors' centre inside it (*open: Mon–Fri 10am–7pm, Sat & Sun 10am–3pm*).

Plaza de Toros
Famously, Ronda is the birthplace of 'modern', that is, on foot, bullfighting, pioneered by legendary matador Pedro Romero in the town's Plaza de Toros in the 18th century.

Today the Plaza is largely a museum, used only once a year in early September for the annual Goyesca *corrida*, or bullfight, that climaxes the September *feria* or fair. Tickets for the Goyesca, in which matadors, picadors and other participants dress in the manner of Goya's paintings of the bullfight, often sell out in advance, and can be expensive, especially to sit in the *sombra* (shade).
Open: Nov–Feb 10am–6pm; Apr–Sept 10am–8pm; Mar & Oct 10am–7pm. Admission charge.

La Ciudad (Old Town)

An anticlockwise route around the old town will lead to the **Palacio de Mondragón**, a renovated Moorish palace now used as town museum, a language school and conference centre (*open: Mon–Fri 10am–7pm, Sat–Sun 10am–3pm. Admission charge*).

Beyond the Mondragón is the handsome **Plaza de Duques de Parcent**, with the unusual arcaded *ayuntamiento* and neighbouring **Santa María la Mayor** church with its Trumpton-baroque bell tower (*open: daily 10am–7pm; admission charge*).

Downhill from the Plaza, calle Armiñan leads to the **Iglesia del Espiritu Santo** (*open: Mon–Sat 10am–1.30pm & 4–7pm; admission charge*). Calle Marques de Salvatierra, off calle Armiñan, leads down to the **Baños Árabes**, the best-preserved Arab baths in Spain (*open: Mon–Fri 10am–7pm, Sat & Sun 10am–3pm*), below the Moorish and Roman bridges that spanned the river before the Puente Nuevo was built in the 18th century.

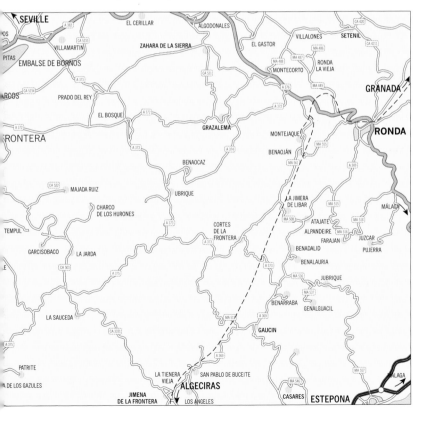

Bullfighting probably originated as a gladiatorial sport, pitting man, mounted or on foot, against a single bull, in Roman or Moorish times. It acquired its layers of robing and ritual – the *traje de luz* (suit of lights) that every matador wears, the *picadores* and *banderilleros* who assist the matador – over the centuries. It was codified in places such as the great equestrian centre Jerez and, later, Ronda in the 18th century, where legendary matador Pedro Romero 'invented' modern, on foot, bullfighting.

The corrida

The *corrida* has its rhythms, which are measured out by the *presidente*, the president of the fight or bullring, and accompanying brass band: it is up to the *presidente* to judge the progress of the *corrida*, and to usher the action on through its three key stages. In the case of a particularly disastrous performance by either matador or bull, he can also dismiss either or both from the ring, to the shame of the former, and the crowd can actually petition for a brave bull to be freed, usually by waving white handkerchiefs.

The first stage of the *corrida*, the *tercio de varas*, is the initial engagement between matador and bull, where the former may leave the bull to the goading of his *peones*, unmounted assistants who taunt the bull with capes. They are joined by *picadores*, mounted on padded horses, who engage the bull by plunging long lances into its spine, weakening its back and neck muscles. It is quite common for their heavily padded and blindfolded horses to be flipped by the enraged bull.

In the *tercio de banderillas*, unmounted assistants, *bandilleros*, often in *trajes de luces* themselves, feint at the bull and plunge *bandilleras* (long beribboned darts) into its back, further weakening the animal.

The final stage – if all goes to plan – is the *estocada*, or death blow, where the matador will judge the bull's strength by various passes of the *muleta*, the famed red cape. The perfect *estocada*, rarely seen, is the *estocada recibiendo*, in which the matador allows the bull to charge, meets it and deals a death blow to the spinal column with his sword. Sometimes, however, especially with younger matadors fighting *novilladas*, the *estocada* is not struck, and it is not uncommon for *peones* to have to finish the bull off with a bolt-gun to the forehead before it is dragged from the *plaza de toros*.

The future of bullfighting

In modern Spain, bullfighting is regarded as something between a sport and an art form. It is reported in the newspapers, highlights are shown on television and matadors are regaled as celebrities on a par with pop and film stars. While only a minority of Spaniards regularly attend bullfights, a majority of

the population seems content to tolerate bullfighting unquestioningly as an inviolable part of Spanish culture, whatever the rest of the world thinks. There are, however, animal rights campaigners who would like to ban bullfighting as cruel and anachronistic, but so far they have not made much progress in winning over public opinion (although the city of Barcelona has declared itself a bullfighting-free zone).

The *corrida*, bullfight, invented in Andalucía, modernised in Ronda, and found all over the region

Arcos to Vejer de la Frontera

Three of Andalucía's larger white towns are closer to the Atlantic than the Costa del Sol and are best approached from the motorway between Algeciras and Jerez. This is also a good route for getting from the western end of Gibraltar or the Costa del Sol to Jerez de la Frontera, Cádiz or Seville. All enjoy impressive sites and are riddled with history.

Iglesia del Divino Salvador, Vejer

Arcos de la Frontera
Arcos is the most impressive of the Pueblos Blancos after Ronda. It too sits on its own defensive bluff, 100m (328ft) above the Rio Guadalete and something of a geological anomaly in the surroundings of gentle rolling farmland.

Arcos's compact *casco antiguo* (old town) is barely a five-minute walk across

Vejer's magnificent Plaza de España fountain

in any direction, but its narrow streets and alleys bulge with marvels over a thousand years old. The **Castillo de los Duques**, named after the family that owned Arcos for centuries, dates back to the 11th century, although its interior is closed to the public. The 15th-century **Iglesia de San Pedro** bell tower has a deafening triple carillon that stops people in their tracks on the hour. The **Convento de la Encarnación** and the **Palacio del Conde de Águila** are among the oldest façades. From Arcos there are two roads east to Ronda. The main road skirts the Embalse de Bornos reservoir, but a more scenic route is over the hills via El Bosque, Benamahoma and Grazalema.

Iglesia de San Pedro, calle Núñez de Prado. Open: Mon–Fri 10.30am–2pm & 5–7pm, Sat 10am–2pm. Closed: Sun. Admission charge.

Medina Sidonia
Medina Sidonia, another hilltop redoubt, is famed as the seat awarded to the family of Guzman el Bueno (the Good), defender of Tarifa (*see pp70–71*).

The Duques de Medina Sidonia continue to oversee the town: the latest incumbent is the firebrand Duchess of Medina Sidonia.

The town's central Plaza de España is home to both an impressive 17th-century *ayuntamiento* (town council) building and Medina's star attraction, the **Iglesia Santa María la Coronada**, which contains some remarkable votary art and details dating back to the period in the 16th century when it also served as local headquarters for the Inquisition. The ruins of Roman sewers, still visible on the outskirts of town, suggest that Medina was an important settlement in pre-Christian times, and its three monumental Moorish gates suggest that it also held similar office prior to the Reconquest.

Iglesia Santa María Coronada, Plaza de la Iglesia Mayor 2. Tel: 956 41 24 04. Open: Mon–Fri 10am–2pm, Sun noon–2pm. Admission charge.

Vejer de la Frontera

It has at least two other rivals for the title, but Vejer has to be one of the, if not the, most exquisite and archetypal of the Pueblos Blancos: a tangle of whitewashed streets and alleys atop a defensive bluff with panoramic views and many of its defences still intact.

Although it has an impressive 16th-century church, the **Iglesia del Divino Salvador**, and parts of the **castle** are also open to the public, the best way to see Vejer is simply to wander its alleys, ramparts and squares, many of them with fantastic views down over the Costa de la Luz. The **Plaza de España** has an outrageous Triana-tiled fountain.

Iglesia del Divino Salvador, calle Ramón y Cajal. Open: daily 10.30am–1.30pm & 7–9pm. Admission charge.
Castillo open: daily 10am–2pm & 5–9pm. Free admission.

Arcos de la Frontera resplendent on its bluff over the Rio Guadalete

Pueblos Blancos

Visiting the Pueblos Blancos, from Seville, Ronda or the Costa del Sol, depends on two things: time and transport. With a car the main *pueblos* could be seen in a couple of days, although the driver would be missing some of the finest landscapes in Andalucía. With time, using public transport and the odd taxi is an ideal way to tour the villages. It's even possible to tour them by cycle or on foot.

Gaucin and its castle

Grazalema
The most visited white town after Ronda and Arcos de la Frontera, Grazalema sits on high ground overlooked by crags. It has the dubious honour of receiving the highest amount of rainfall in Spain, but at least that keeps the countryside green. The town is attractive in itself and serves as a base for hiking in the nature reserve named after it (*see pp86–7*), which is good for birdwatching and botanising.

Artesanía Textil de Grazalema keeps up the local weaving industry, making blankets and ponchos on hand looms in its small factory, which can be visited. *Carretera de Ronda. Open: Mon–Thur 8am–2pm & 3–6.30pm, Fri 8am–2pm. Closed: Aug.*

Zahara de las Sierras
A car is necessary to reach the breathtaking Puerta de las Palomas (Pass of the Doves) above Grazalema. From here you can look down on little-visited Zahara de las Sierras, on its windswept peak overlooking a vast *embalse*, or reservoir. The obligatory ruined Moorish castle at the top of Zahara's

craggy pinnacle is the best preserved in the region, with 360-degree views.

Setenil de las Bodegas
A roundabout but picturesque route from Zahara leads across country to the strangest of the Pueblos Blancos: Setenil de las Bodegas.

Where the great majority of Pueblos Blancos were built on inaccessible bluffs for defensive reasons before and during the Moorish presence and the Reconquest, Setenil was built over caves hidden in the valley of the Rio Trejo, first inhabited in pre-Christian times. Today, its houses seem to emerge from the rock, and many have olive groves on their roofs.

Olvera
North of Setenil, Olvera is interesting for its church, and its reputation as one of the worst 19th-century bandit lairs.

Gaucin
Southwest of Ronda, the A-369 leads to another pretty town, Gaucin. These barren mountainscapes proved ideal hiding places for fugitive Moors during

the Reconquest, and many of the villages here bear the prefix 'Ben' – Benadalid, Benalauria, Benarraba – from the Arabic *ibn* (son of). Gaucin is now a sizeable artists' colony.

Casares

Below Gaucin, on another peak between the village and the coast, is tiny Casares. Another classic tangle of whitewashed alleys on a mountain peak, it is notable chiefly as the birthplace of Blas Infante, the founder of the Andalucismo regional autonomy movement in the 1930s.

Jimena de la Frontera

West beyond Gaucin, before the sierras flatten out towards Gibraltar, is the pleasant hill town of Jimena de la Frontera, with another fortress from the centuries of the Reconquest.

To the north and southwest of Gaucin and Jimena is the remote expanse of the Parque Natural Los Alcornocales, a nature reserve that includes the biggest extension of cork trees in Spain – their bark being harvested to make bottle corks. There are visitor centres for the reserve at Alcalá de los Gazules and Cortes de la Frontera.

The rooftops of Grazalema, the most dramatic Pueblo Blanco and wettest town in Spain

Los bandoleros (bandits)

As recently as the 1950s the mountains of the Serrania de Ronda were still known as bandit country, although these bandits were a somewhat different breed from the highwaymen of the 18th and 19th centuries. The treacherous mountain routes between Algeciras and Gibraltar and the cities of Seville, Málaga and Granada had long been favoured by *contrabandistas*, smugglers, bringing illicit supplies ashore and spiriting them through the high mountain passes. In the 1940s and 50s, the bandits shared the mountain paths with fugitive 'Reds', soldiers of the defeated Republican brigades fleeing the vengeance of Franco's henchmen after the Civil War (*see pp100–101*) and eking out an existence at these inhospitable altitudes.

Banditry probably first appeared in Andalucía around the 12th century, where we might date the decisive swing in favour of the Christians during the long centuries of the Reconquest. These first bandits were fugitive Moors fleeing persecution, or at least forced conversion. By the 18th century, with the majority of Moors either assimilated or expelled, the bandits tended to be disenfranchised or disgruntled peasants or disgraced gentry forced to flee into the hills after committing murders or other hanging offences. The Pueblos Blancos were notorious bandit lairs, including Gaucin and, most notorious of all, Olvera, which actually features in a famous saying of the period: 'Kill your man and flee to Olvera.'

Perhaps inevitably, many of these figures acquired a romantic, Robin Hood-like, status, and their system of exacting money from the unwary rich if they ventured unwisely into the mountains would certainly have struck a welcome chord with the region's poor. One such, José Alloa Tragabuches, was a famous Ronda bullfighter and a pupil

of Pedro Romero (*see p74*). Myths about Tragabuches vary: in one he killed a rival matador and fled justice, while in another he killed an unfaithful wife or girlfriend in a fit of jealous rage and headed for Olvera.

Another bandit, José María Hinojosa Cabacho, nicknamed El Tempranillo, was a media legend in his own time, and was even given to issuing his own press releases, once declaring that while the king might rule Spain, El Tempranillo ruled the sierras. When wealthy northern Europeans began to tour Andalucía in the 19th century, figures such as El Tempranillo were even contacted by rich tourists willing to pay for the thrill of being 'held up' by a bona fide bandit. And when El Tempranillo married a young woman from (and in) Grazalema, the authorities are said to have turned a blind eye while the nuptials took place.

The romantic form of banditry began to die out in the mid-19th century, due largely to drastic measures taken by the state. However, for a long time after the Civil War had ended and even when democracy had returned to Spain, rumours kept circulating about ageing, renegade 'Red' soldiers hiding out in the sierras, living off the land and avoiding the Guardia Civil, unaware that hostilities were over. Fact or myth, it all makes for some good stories. The lives and reputations, histories and legends, of all the rogues, rovers, fugitives and folk-heroes who lived and died in the sierras are celebrated in a museum in Ronda, the Museo del Bandolero (*Calle Armiñán. Tel: 952 87 77 85; www.museobandolero.com. Open: daily, 10.30am–8pm. Admission charge*).

Facing page: The barren Serranía mountains
Above: Entrance to the Bandit Museum in Ronda

Walk: Benaoján to Jimera de Libar

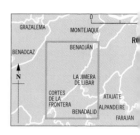

This spectacular walk along the Rio Guadiaro valley is one of the most accessible off-road walks in the region, suitable for a morning or shady late afternoon walk, and with transport and refreshment options at either end.
Allow 2–3 hours.

Benaoján is accessible from Ronda by bus, rail or a gentle 6km (3³/₄ mile) downhill track through farmland. Ideally this should be a morning walk begun from Benaoján, with the added proviso that the route, on rough paths above the river bank, should not be attempted in inclement weather or by the uncertain solo walker. The perfect itinerary, possible from either starting point, would either end or pause for lunch at Benaoján's El Molino del Santo hotel's lovely garden restaurant, under willows by a waterfall feeding the Rio Guadiaro.

1 Benaoján station

The route proper begins at and across the traffic level crossing at the far end of Benaoján station. Signs for the path lead right, off the road and into open countryside.

2 Riverside track

You'll find yourself on a rough but substantial dirt track following the river to your right and with the Ronda–Algeciras railway line elevated above it, also on your right. The path rises and falls from a few feet to a

hundred or so feet above the river bank, with no major diversions and only two minor tributaries to ford by stepping stone or rudimentary wooden bridge.
Halfway through the route, just past a ruined farmhouse on the left, you'll be faced by a fork, but in fact both routes continue on to the destination.

3 Cueva de la Pileta

This is an idler's walk, with plenty of spots to stop for a snack or breather, or to take in the fantastic mountain views. The Cueva de la Pileta is visited by an atmospheric hour-long guided tour (*departures from entrance, reached via road MA501, when sufficient numbers of people have gathered to form a group, daily 10am–1pm and 4–6pm; admission charge*). Inside there are superb prehistoric paintings and what appears to be an ancient form of writing, the origins and purposes of which have yet to be explained.

4 Quercus restaurant

Nearing Jimera, the path passes a derelict riverside café and then crosses the tracks, to pass behind the Quercus restaurant (recommended) on the Jimera railway platform.

Rail connections can be used to return to Benaoján or Ronda for lunch (although currently not onward to Cortes and the Gecko, but it's worth a cab). Train times can change, so consult an up-to-date RENFE timetable.

There are also a number of extensions, *one a diversion of a matter of minutes, two others long enough to extend this route into a full day ramble, worth considering before you plan your itinerary.*

5 Estación Cortes de la Frontera

From Jimera, you can continue on a slightly shorter riverside hike to Estación Cortes de la Frontera and its riverside Hotel El Gecko.

Allow 2¹/₂ hours extra.

6 El Gato

Just outside Benaoján on the road towards Ronda, accessible across the rail line, is the dramatic El Gato cave system, its entrance is open to all (*free*), but its depths are the preserve of the experienced cave diver.

7 La Venta Vega

Serious walkers might also want to consider prefacing the Benaoján–Jimera stretch with the stroll from La Venta Vega restaurant on the Seville road downhill (after the first kilometre) through breathtaking mountain passes and valleys to Benaoján itself.

Allow 2¹/₂ hours extra.

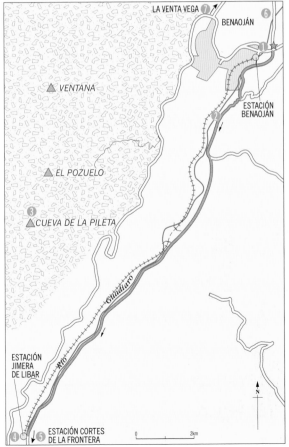

The limestone bedrock of the area of mountains now protected as the Parque Natural Sierra de Grazalema, and its position equidistant between the Atlantic and Mediterranean, has given rise to a unique and vulnerable combination of geology, flora and fauna. The park covers 52,000 hectares (130,000 acres), roughly bounded by the towns of El Bosque, Algodonales, Ronda and Cortes de la Frontera, and merges to the southwest with the Parque Natural Los Alcornocales (see p81).

Star of the park's flora and fauna is *Abies pinsapo*, the Spanish fir tree (*pinsapo* in Spanish), which only grows above 1,000m (3,280ft) and is a relic of the forests of the Tertiary era. Far more spectacular are the eagles which fly over the mountains, but the most conspicuous bird you are likely to see, still impressive as it soars on thermal currents of air, is the griffon vulture.

Other wildlife living here includes kestrels, owls, ibex, otters, snakes, lizards and other reptiles – some of them rare. Botanists will find a wealth of interesting flowers, particularly orchids.

Where to go

You can get a glimpse of the scenery and perhaps the wildlife through a car window, especially if you stop at one of the viewpoints which are located at Cintillo (Benaocaz, near Ubrique), Puerto de las Palomas and Puerto de los Acebuches (both near Grazalema); but you will perhaps enjoy your visit more if you follow one of the 15 marked walking routes. The most popular is to Garganta Verde, a gorge popular with canyoners and home to a colony of vultures. The footpath following the old road between Grazalema and Benamahoma, over the Puerto de las Cumbres, takes you past some fine woods of Spanish fir.

Other good places to visit in the park are the botanic garden at El Castillejo (El Bosque) and the Museo del Agua (Water Museum) in an old water mill at Benamahoma.

Rules and precautions

The Parque Natural Sierra de Grazalema is one of the most accessible of Andalucía's nature reserves, but it is very sensitive to visitor interference and as such is patrolled by wardens. Always keep to marked paths, do not remove plants or even rocks, and leave any animals you come across alone, particularly during the breeding season. And never light a fire: even though these hills receive a high level of rainfall, forest fire is still an ever-present risk.

Information and guided tours
There are four visitor centres for the park (in addition to Grazalema tourist information office):
Ronda: *Palacio de Mondragón Ronda. Tel: 952 87 11 71.*
Cortes de la Frontera: *Avenida de la Democracia. Tel: 952 15 45 99.*
El Bosque (useful if coming from the direction of Arcos de la Frontera): *Avenida de la Diputación. Tel: 956 72 70 29.*
Zahara de la Sierra: *Plaza de Zahara 3. Tel: 956 12 31 14.*

Two private companies based in Grazalema organise walks and excursions, ranging from easy to difficult:
Horizon: *Calle Corrales Terceros 29. Tel: 956 13 23 63; www.horizonaventura.com*
Pinzapo: *Calle Las Piedras 11. Tel: 956 13 21 66.*

The wilder parts of Grazalema's park are tightly controlled by the park authorities

Costa del Sol

Although it has been a synonym for the worst excesses of holiday development for almost 40 years, it would be snobbish and lazy simply to dismiss the Costa del Sol out of hand. Parts are blighted by unregulated sprawl, but the 21st-century first-time visitor may be surprised at how much of it remains free of intense high-rise development. And it is noticeable in some places that the Costa del Sol is attracting and providing facilities for a new, discerning, more eco-minded class of tourist.

Marbella palms

The Costa del Sol stretches from La Linea de la Concepción, on the border with Gibraltar, to Nerja, east of Málaga.

Estepona
The first stop of note, this is a fairly low-key resort with a big expatriate community, but still a working Spanish town. Away from the busy seafront, much of the town centre is pedestrian, with lateral boulevards and cobbled streets that run between two pleasant squares, Plaza las Flores and Plaza Arces. The town has a busy modernist Plaza de Toros, which hosts occasional concerts given by international artists touring Spain, and below it by the lighthouse a marina whose bars and clubs are less desperately trendy than those in Puerto Banús. Casares and the nearer Pueblos Blancos (*see pp80–81*) are a short drive or bus ride north.

San Pedro de Alcantara
Landlocked a kilometre away from its beach en route to Marbella, this is still a pleasant little Spanish town, with

pedestrian streets and the handsome Plaza de la Iglesia where townsfolk promenade. It is also the main shopping centre for the booming *urbanizaciones*, gated housing developments, nearby, with multilingual bookshops and newsstands, restaurants and stores.

Mijas
Fuengirola on the coast is an unattractive package holiday resort and service centre, mainly useful for its train station; Mijas, a few kilometres behind it, is another story. A pretty old town now all but taken over by foreign residents, it is a nice place to escape from the beaches, apartment blocks and traffic for a stroll or a leisurely lunch.

Torremolinos
Torremolinos is currently living down a reputation as a beer and beach resort, and the authorities are following Marbella's model in town gentrification, with replanted squares and pedestrian areas. It remains a big nightlife resort.

Benalmadena

Many of Torremolinos's quieter tourist attractions, such as Sea Life and the Tivoli *parque tematico* (theme park), are in this satellite town, which has a cable-car system up into the hills overlooking the town. The *pueblo* proper of Benalmadena, a few kilometres inland, is surprisingly unspoilt.

Marbella's Paseo Maritimo, a favourite stroll for townsfolk and visitors alike

Marbella and Puerto Banús

Marbella became a magnet for the jet set in the late 1950s and early 1960s, and with the advent of mass market travel established itself as perhaps the most high-class resort on Spain's Mediterranean littoral. The intervening decades have been something of a roller-coaster ride for the resort and its smaller sibling, the marina playground of Puerto Banús 4km (2¹/₂ miles) to the west.

Marbella's medieval fortifications

Spain's laid-back attitude to international extradition treaties at this time also made it a haven for north European criminals and their booty – as well, alas, as their murderous feuds. Marbella's reputation nosedived after a series of particularly gruesome murders, and only in recent decades has it begun to claw back some of its earlier glamour.

Two men have left a particular legacy in modern-day Marbella: Prince Alfonso von Hohenlohe, an Austrian aristocrat with Mexican connections who built the Marbella Club Hotel in the 1950s, and the former mayor, controversial right-wing business tycoon and boss of Atlético Madrid football club, Jesus Gil y Gil.

Marbella is an immensely attractive place to visit. It has a handsome seafront promenade, now lined with restaurants, and its lovely old Alameda, shaded by aged palms, gives on to a high-tech *rambla* decorated with Salvador Dalí bronzes.

Casco Antiguo (Old Town)

The *casco antiguo* (old town) has been exquisitely refurbished, nowhere more so than in Plaza de los Naranjos (square of the orange trees), where the 17th-century *ayuntamiento* building overlooks some of the priciest bars in town. In fact, the whitewashed alleys and squares of the *casco* would give any of the Pueblos Blancos a run for their money.

The streets are full of handsome, well-kept buildings and interesting details, and half the fun is wandering around them without particularly heading anywhere. Highlights include the 16th-century Iglesia de la Encarnación, the pretty Plaza de Altamirano, the Renaissance Palacio Bazán and the walls of the old Arab castle.

Museo del Grabado Contemporáneo

Hidden in an alleyway behind the Iglesia de la Encarnación is the small but impressive Museum of Contemporary Prints, housed in a Renaissance mansion originally built as a hospital. It has a sizeable collection of Mirós, some smaller works by Picasso, and a feisty policy of showcasing contemporary art. The building itself, on four floors, is worth the entry fee alone and is being expanded. The museum is close by the remnants of the Moorish ramparts to the city.

Calle Hospital Bazán. Open: Tue–Sat 10am–2pm & 6–9pm. Admission charge.

Puerto Banús

This famous marina has long been a tourist attraction in its own right, although mainly for gawpers naively expecting a glimpse of celebrity millionaires. The boats are fun to look at (at any time, there must be half a billion euros moored in Puerto Banús), as are their owner, and there are numerous good if expensive seafood and American restaurants – and even an Indian one – on the quay. But Puerto Banús still has the slightly dislocated air of something that has just landed here from outer space.

The Plaza de los Naranjos, the prettiest square in the beautiful casco antiguo

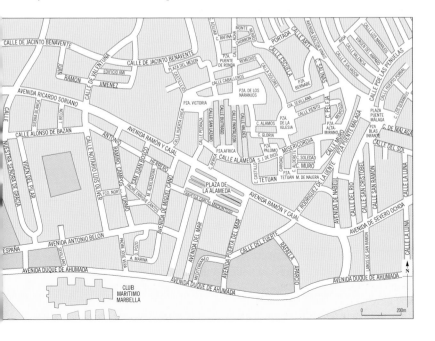

Nerja and the Costa Tropical

East of Málaga, the Costa del Sol is much less heavily developed than the Torremolinos–Estepona stretch, although the coast is filling up fast with new apartments and hotels, and the hills are being covered with private villas. The only major resorts along it are the relatively restrained Rincón de la Victoria, Torre del Mar and Nerja. Beyond Nerja, the Costa del Sol comes to an end and the topography changes abruptly into the heavily indented and very attractive Costa Tropical, the coast of Granada province, thus named because of the orchards of tropical fruit that fill its valleys.

Salobreña church tower

Nerja

Nerja is a growing, but still fairly low-rise, resort popular with foreign tourists, built around a viewing platform jutting over the Mediterranean (the Balcón de Europa). It has sparse historical or cultural interest, but outside the town is a cave – the Cueva de Nerja, styled as the 'Costa del Sol's natural cathedral' – which is used as the venue for an international festival of music and dance in the summer. A short way inland from Nerja is the well-kept **Frigiliana**, certainly a contender for the prettiest town in Spain.

The Axarquia

The hills behind Vélez-Málaga and Nerja, a region called the Axarquia, are extremely picturesque and dotted with pretty villages. The convoluted contours mean that getting around here is slow and time-consuming; public transport is limited and a car is really the only way

to see the sights. The colourful, wine-producing town of **Cómpeta** is the de-facto capital of upland Axarquia. In the valleys below it are two villages, **Archez** and **Salares**, in which the church towers are the undisguised Mudéjar brick minarets of mosques, dating from the 15th and 13th centuries respectively. A separate journey takes you up a twisting road to **Comares**, a pretty town perched on a rocky peak from which there are prodigious views.

The Costa Tropical

The resorts of Granada province's coastline are mainly popular with Spanish holidaymakers, but they are gradually being discovered by foreign tourists and homeowners. The extension of the coastal motorway from Málaga and the completion of the motorway down the valley from Granada are likely to open them up further to the same internationalisation that has affected the Costa del Sol.

The two largest towns are the port of **Motril** and the resort of **Almuñécar**, founded by the Phoenicians, which sits under an Arab castle. In between them is **Salobreña**, which manages to be both a laid-back holiday resort and a typical Andalucían white town swarming over a great rock above the sea. There's a stiff walk up through the narrow streets to the castle, but you'll feel compensated for it by the view from the battlements.

The Costa Tropical's best beach is that contained by the horseshoe bay of **La Herradura** and checked in both directions by massive headlands beneath which are some of the best waters for scuba diving on the coast of Spain. The dive school in La Herradura's pretty harbour, Marina del Este, can take you on a brief tour of the seabed.

The aqueduct at Nerja

Málaga

Andalucía's second largest city after Seville, with a population of over half a million, Málaga is the main airport of entry for visitors, the administrative centre for most government agencies, and the place where you will find overseas consulates or their representatives. Many people fly into and out of Málaga for a holiday on the Costa del Sol without bothering to visit the city itself, but it merits at least a half day's exploration.

Málaga's one-armed lady

Málaga's history stretches back to the Phoenicians, who established it as a key Mediterranean port, a role it has kept through Moorish and Christian rule until the present day. The Phoenicians also introduced viniculture, which blossomed with the city's sweet and fortified wines, but the industry was devastated by the 19th-century phylloxera epidemic. (The Larios family did better with their Málaga-distilled gin, which still beats famous British brands in blindfold tests.)

The city gave Spain and indeed the 20th century its most famous painter, Picasso, and it was the second most fought-over Republican bulwark after Barcelona during the Civil War.

The city centre, bordered by the river-bed, Alameda Principal, Carreteria Alamos and Alcazaba, is a busy clutch of streets and alleys. Málaga also claims to be a city of gardens, its main one being the Paseo del Parque.

Alcazaba

The city centre is overlooked by this fortress-palace that is entered through a series of horseshoe-shaped arched gateways. Next to it is an excavated Roman theatre. There are reasonably good views over the city from the walls of the Alcazaba, but much better ones from the castle that stands above it on the crest of the hill, Gibralfaro.
Alcazaba, Calle Alcazabilla. Open: summer Tue–Sun 9.30am–8pm; winter Tue–Sun 8.30am–7pm. Gibralfaro, either walk or take bus 35 or, by car, follow the signs from Plaza del General Torrijos. Open: 9am–8pm (closes 6pm in winter). Combined admission charge for both monuments.

Museo Picasso

Picasso left Málaga when he was ten years old, but this hasn't deterred the city from celebrating its most famous son as if he had a lifelong attachment to his place of birth. The house where he was born and briefly lived (Casa Natal) on Plaza de la Merced has been turned into a gallery for exhibitions related to Picasso's work, but if you are at all curious about the man and his art you will want to make straight for the Museo

Picasso in the former Palacio de Buenavista, which has a permanent collection of 155 works donated by the artist's daughter-in-law and grandson. In the basement of the building are the remains of a Phoenician house and two towers dating back to the 6th century BC or earlier.

Calle San Agustin 8. Open: Tue–Sun 10am–8pm (closes 9pm on Fri and Sat). Admission charge but free on last Sun of month after 3pm.

Catedral

Málaga's cathedral is low on architectural detail but big on imposing presence: it's the size of a small mountain.

A hotchpotch of Gothic, Renaissance and baroque, it is made odder by the absence of one of its towers (funds were diverted to Spain's war chest), which earned it the nickname La Manquita, the One-Armed Lady.

Calle Molina Lario. Open: Mon–Sat 10am–6.45pm. Admission charge.

The Alcazaba seen from the Alameda

Few artists can hope to generate controversies extending beyond their lifetimes, but more than 30 years after his death Pablo Ruiz Picasso still manages to upset people's notions of what constitutes art.

Picasso was born in Málaga's Plaza de la Merced in 1881 to artistic parents – his father was a teacher, and it was under his influence that Picasso began painting in his early teens. As even his mid-teen self-portraits and other exercises – most of them conventional

representational works – showed, he had a precocious skill and eye for the different.

His father was appointed to Barcelona's La Lonja art school in 1895, and Picasso was accepted as an exceptional student the following year. Within a matter of years he had been adopted as the mascot of Barcelona's *modernista* avant-garde that met at the Els Quatre Gats (Four Cats) bar. By 1897, he was studying at the Royal Academy in Madrid and already attracting critical attention. Toulouse-Lautrec and Cézanne were influences on his work, and the latter would continue to influence him along with Gauguin and other fauvists (primitives).

Picasso began his first distinctive work, what was later called his 'blue period', in 1901, when he was barely 20, a period typified by works such as *The Old Guitarist* (1903). Like the subsequent 'rose period', while accurate in terms of material and chronologically verifiable, this was not part of a traditional career trajectory, of an artist experimenting or developing. Picasso already knew what he wanted to do, and how he wanted to portray things. Like his next, almost literally shattering, change of

The spa town of Lanjarón, source of Spain's most popular bottled water

Architecture

One of the most appealing aspects of the Alpujarras is the vernacular architecture that echoes the Berber architecture of North Africa. The typical house of the Alpujarras is built of stone and has a flat roof spread with an impermeable layer of gravel, from which sprouts a tall, capped chimney. The villages are complicated clusters of such houses, each stuck to its neighbours, with erratic narrow, stepped and tapering streets squeezing between them.

The High Alpujarras

There's only one twisting road through the scenic part of the Alpujarras, with spurs to any villages not directly on it, so you won't get lost. The downside is that you'll have to double back to return to your starting point or make a lengthy loop, curving around endless mountainsides. To start a tour, take the motorway from Granada towards the coast and turn off for the spa of Lanjarón. Just before Órgiva, the main market town of the western Alpujarras, a road ascends towards the High Alpujarras. There is a bus service to the main villages of the Alpujarras from Granada. In recent years a number of comfortable and charming hotels have opened in the Alpujarras, making this a good place to escape if you are in need of peace and fresh air.

Espantabrujas, 'witch-scarers', are common in mountain villages

Lanjarón
Famed throughout Spain as the source of the bottled spring water sold in every Spanish supermarket, Lanjarón has been a centre of population and a renowned spa since Roman times. The *balneario*, or spa, is on its one main street, Avenida Andalucía, and in summer months throngs with people.

O Sel Ling
On the way up to the High Alpujarras there is a turning from a mountain pass to this Tibetan Buddhist retreat centre, but you will need to follow a minor road and then a track for 7km (4¹/₂ miles). It is open to visitors from 3–6pm each afternoon.

Poqueira valley
By far the most attractive part of the Alpujarras – and the most popular – is the higher part of the **Barranco de Poqueira** (Poqueira valley). Here there are three villages; the lowest of them, which the road passes through first, is **Pampaneira**. As you continue to climb past it you will get a good view of the flat-roofed houses and their idiosyncratic chimneys.

Bubión and **Capileira** are reached by a detour from the main road. Both are attractive places to take a stroll and make good bases for a few days' walking. Beyond Capileira the road continues towards the summits of the Sierra Nevada, and you can take a minibus excursion from the Sierra Nevada National Park visitors' centre to the peaks above.

La Taha
Round another few corners from the Poqueira Valley is another group of

villages known collectively as La Taha. The two prettiest are down the slope, **Mecina Fondales** and **Ferreirola**. **Pitres**, meanwhile, is a larger town on the main road.

Trevelez

Spain's highest village (at 1,476m/ 4,843ft) uses its altitude to dry-cure hams that are renowned throughout Andalucía. From here the scenery of the Alpujarras becomes less attractive and the villages less interesting, so this is a good place to turn around if you don't want to do a lot more driving. If you want to make a circular tour of the Alpujarras, continue past Trevelez and take one of the next two turnings right (south), either of which will bring you to the small wine-producing town of Torvizcón and thus back to Órgiva and the road out of the Alpujarras via Lanjarón. A much longer route is to continue on the main road towards Almería and cross the Sierra Nevada by the Puerto de la Ragua pass, which brings you on to a motorway back to Granada.

Rocky outcrop in the Alpujarras

Walk: Capileira and the High Alpujarras

This is one of the easier walks in the High Alpujarras. It starts at the centre of the pretty mountain village of Capileira – and can be pursued as far as mood, stamina or weather dictate. It also begins at above 1,400m (4,593ft) above sea level, with only a minimal climb up the Poqueira Gorge to the power station above it.

Allow half a day or less.

1 Capileira
The walk begins in the village centre, heading downhill towards the river. The lowest bridge crosses the river outside the village and is named on some maps Puente Chiscar. This will lead you up through the steep cultivated hillsides above Capileira.

2 Poqueira Gorge
The path continues for 4km (2 $^1/_2$ miles) or so (*on this terrain, estimate a walking duration of 1 $^1/_2$ hours for this*) before you meet the path leading up the Poqueira Gorge to the hydroelectric power station installed many years ago on the Rio Poqueira.

Capileira and the snows of the Sierra Nevada in the distance

3 Return to Capileira

From here you have a variety of options. Crossing over the river you'll encounter a dirt path that will lead you back to Capileira. Continue to the hydroelectric plant and a path at a fork below it will also lead you back down to Capileira.

Other walks from Capileira

There are plenty of other options for walks starting from Capileira. One obvious one is to go down the Poqueira valley instead of up it, passing Bubión to reach Poqueira and eventually Órgiva in the valley (with the option of taking a bus back). From the Poqueira valley you can also walk west to the Buddhist retreat of O Sel Ling, Soportújar and Carataunas, and east through La Taha to distant Trevelez. These east–west walks form part of the the the 1,280km (795-mile) GR7 (E4) 'Mediterranean Arc' long-distance footpath that ultimately connects the Aegean Sea with the Atlantic Ocean.

With expert guidance and equipment, Capileira can also be used as a base for an attempt on **Mulhacén**, the highest peak (3,480m/11,417ft) in the entire Iberian peninsula. This is best done over a period of days, with local accommodation arranged from Capileira or Órgiva. Every year on 5 August the sturdier villagers embark on their own walk, an annual *romeria*, or religious procession, to the hermitage of La Virgen de las Nieves (the Virgin of the Snows), near the summit of Mulhacén. However, this should not be attempted by anyone uncertain about either their ability to climb the largest mountain in Spain or their head for heights.

Almería province

The easternmost province of Andalucía is a dry region that includes Europe's only desert. Its mountain ranges, ravines and badland landscapes can be stark and fascinating if you like to feel you are off the beaten track, but Almería has other attractions if you want them.

Almería's dusty interior

The first impression of Almería for many visitors, however, is not of unspoilt nature but of a sea of plastic sheeting. Warm winter temperatures here have encouraged farmers to turn their fields into vast greenhouses in order to supply northern European supermarkets with out-of-season vegetables.

The capital city, Almería, may not be high on anyone's must-see list, but it does have an impressive *alcazaba* (castle) and the streets below are full of tapas bars. There are other sights scattered around the province, but above all it is the austere natural scenery that strikes the visitor. Sea and desert meet on the beautiful unspoilt beaches of the east coast, where you can escape the crowds.

South coast

Almería's southern coast is geographically an extension of the Costa del Sol and Costa Tropical, but much of it is unattractively swathed in the plastic greenhouses that have made many farmers millionaires, particularly around the boom town of El Ejido. The coast's main town is **Adra** and its biggest resorts are **Almerimar**, **Roquetas del Mar** and **Aguadulce**.

East coast

Very different in character is the east coast of the province. In recent years, unchecked resort sprawl has made a mess of a beautiful line of beaches from **Carboneras** to beyond **Garrucha**, although some inaccessible coves have so far escaped the developers. The resort of **Mojácar** is as bad as the rest, but it still has a pretty town centre perched on a hill a little way inland. South of Carboneras, much of the coast has survived intact. The headland of **Cabo de Gata** is a nature reserve (*see pp112–13*).

Inland Almería

Tabernas is the most popular inland destination in Almería because of its Wild West theme parks, chief among them Mini-Hollywood, which remain from the days when spaghetti westerns were shot around here. Near it is an experimental solar power station, and not much further away is **Los Millares**, the excavated and partially restored settlement of a Copper Age civilisation.

Towards the coast is **Sorbas** and a hidden beauty spot and nature reserve of gypsum karst scenery. **Níjar**, in the hills between Sorbas and Cabo de Gata, is famed for its pottery. There are good views of Almería and its coast from the

Water and nautical sculpture where Almería's elegant *rambla* reaches the seafront

roads crossing two mountain ranges, the Sierra de los Filabres (passing by Calar Alto observatory) and the Sierra de Gádor (via Enix). The valley on the north side of Gádor leads into the Alpujarras (*see pp102–3*).
Mini-Hollywood, Carretera Nacional

N-340. Tel: 950 36 52 36. Open: Tue–Sun 10am–9pm (until 7pm in winter).
Wild West shows at 12 noon and 5pm.
Admission charge.
Los Millares, Santa Fe de Mondujar.
Tel: 677 90 34 04. Open: Wed–Sun 10am–2pm. Free admission.

Almería: the city

The least visited of Andalucía's regional capitals, this thriving port has much to recommend it to the visitor. It may lack the grand monuments of Seville and Granada, but there's plenty to explore, culture old and new, few of the crowds and hassles of the big cities, and a lively nightlife.

City and old town from the sea

Almería, from the Arabic *al-mariya* (mirror of the sea), was a major port from the earliest days of the Moorish presence in Andalucía until their expulsion. City and region were severely damaged by an earthquake in 1522 and languished in poverty until the mid-20th century, when efforts began to revive agriculture and develop tourism. Despite the quake, some impressive sights remain, as do handsome examples of later architecture.

Alcazaba

This great Arab fortress is on three levels, with ongoing excavations, gardens and water courses and spectacular views all the way up to the Torre del Homeiaje added by the Christian reconquerors of the city. From the second enclosure there are views over the **Centro Rescate de la Fauna Sahariana** (Centre for the Rescue of Saharan Fauna), a research centre where endangered gazelles from the western Sahara are bred in captivity. It can be visited, but only by prior appointment (*tel: 950 28 10 45*). *Calle Almanzor. Open: Tue–Sun 9am–8.30pm. Admission charge (EU citizens free).*

Old Town

The old town between the Alcazaba, the Rambla de Beléi and the port boasts some very fine local architecture with a wealth of eccentric detail. Particularly recommended is **La Plaza Vieja**, also known as Plaza de la Constitución, on which stands the town hall clock.

If you don't care for monuments, come back at night when the old town is alive with bar hoppers: by tradition, each drink in Almería comes with a complimentary tapa.

Cable Inglés

By far the most conspicuous of the city's monuments is a piece of industrial archaeology. The Cable Inglés is a great, hulking railway pier running briefly into the sea, which was built between 1902 and 1904 by a British company (Inglés is Spanish for 'English') to load ore on to waiting ships.

Catedral

Almería's cathedral sits in a stately square and shares its Gothic architecture, and architect Diego de Sileó, with the cathedral at Granada. The neo-primitive sun icon on its east (dawn-facing) wall has been read as evidence of freemasonry among 16th-century clergy, and is used as a logo by the city.

Plaza de la Catedral. Open: Mon–Fri 10am–5pm, Sat 10am–1pm. Admission charge.

Centro Andaluz de la Fotografía

Housed in a sedate 18th-century building, the Centro Andaluz de la Fotografía has a high reputation for its exhibitions of comtemporary and journalistic photography.

Calle Conde Ofalía 30. Open: Mon–Fri 9am–2pm & 4–9pm, Sat 6–9pm.

Museo de Almería

The province's purpose-built archaeological museum focuses on the two civilisations of Los Millares and El Algar, with 900 exhibits drawn from a collection of 80,000 items. The largest piece is a 13m (43ft) high column that rises through the three levels of the museum.

Plaza de Barcelona (opposite the bus and train station). Tel: 950 26 61 12. Open: Mon 6–9pm, Tue–Sat 11am–2pm & 6–8pm, Sun 11am–2pm. Admission charge.

Almería's Alcazaba above the old town

Walk: Cabo de Gata

Just over half an hour's drive or bus ride east of Almería city, Cabo de Gata is a dramatic volcanic headland and nature reserve that offers clean air, excellent views and unspoilt beaches. This walk begins at the fishing village and low-rise resort of San Miguel de Cabo de Gata. If you arrive by car you'll have to double back from the cape, but if you come by bus you can take another one back from San José at the end of an exhilarating hike along some of Spain's finest coastal scenery.

For bus information, ask at Almería bus station or contact Autocares Becera (*Almería to San Miguel de Cabo de Gata; tel: 950 22 44 03*) or Autocares Bernardo (*San José to Almería; tel: 950 25 04 22; www.autocaresbernardo.com*).
Allow a whole day's walking (a good 6 hours) to get to the cape and back, or to reach San José (24km/15 miles).

1 Torre de San Miguel
From the martello tower in Cabo de Gata head southeast (left facing the sea) towards the Salinas del Cabo de Gata.

2 Salinas de Cabo de Gata
These working salt pans, stretching between the town and Playa de la Fabriquilla, are a haven for indigenous and migratory birds, including, in season, flocks of flamingos and avocets, except in winter, when the pans are drained and harvested. Much of the salt industry is based at Las Salinas and La Almadraba de Monteleva, 6km (4 miles) from the El Cabo resort.

3 Playa de la Fabriquilla
At Playa de la Fabriquilla, the flat plains give way to the Sierra del Cabo hills, few of them above 400m (1,312ft) but dramatic in this setting.

The Cabo de Gata lighthouse

4 Faro de Cabo de Gata

The path (bike as well as foot) here joins the coast road and begins to rise up towards the cape itself, with its Faro (lighthouse) de Cabo de Gata perched on 200m (656ft) high cliffs. There is an information point and magnificent *miradors* (viewing platforms), with varied views, a short stroll from the car park. At roughly 12km (7^1/$_2$ miles) from El Cabo de Gata resort, this is the spot to consider your options.

5 Mónsul and Los Genoveses

If you are going to continue rather than return to San Miguel de Cabo de Gata the way you came, follow the track beyond the lighthouse above the cliffs, which passes through a gate blocking the way to traffic. After the watchtower of La Vela Blanca you drop down to two beautiful beaches, the Playa de Mónsul (used in a key scene in the film *Indiana Jones and the Last Crusade*) and the Playa de los Genoveses to reach the resort and principal settlement of the Cabo de Gata, San José.

6 San José

This expanding but still not over-sized resort has ample hotels and restaurants, and makes a good place to stay for the night if you don't want to rush back to Almería.

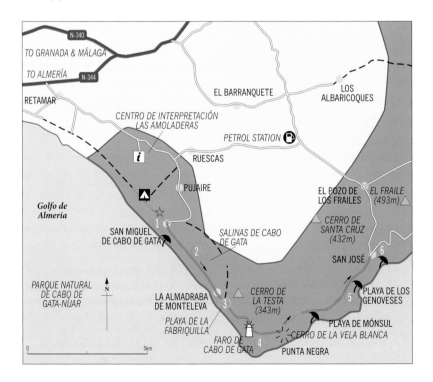

Granada: the city

Dominated by the sprawling Alhambra but with a wealth of other monuments within easy walking distance of the base of the Alhambra hill, Granada is an ideal city for strollers. It's barely one-third the size of Seville, with a similar population ratio, but has a culture to rival that of its larger sibling. Granada's sights are concentrated in three areas: the hill of the Alhambra (*see pp116–19*), the facing hill of the Albaicín (*see pp120–21*) and the city centre around the cathedral.

Granada glimpsed from the Palacios

El Bañuelo

These exquisite Arab baths were built in the 11th century and thus predate the finest parts of the Alhambra.
Carrera del Darro 31. Tel: 958 02 78 00. Open: Tue–Sat 10am–2pm. Free admission.

Catedral and Capilla Real

Granada's mountainous cathedral, begun by Diego de Siloé in the 16th century but only completed in the 18th, is, despite its size, decidedly modest in its interior. Light and airy, thanks to its 27m (88¹/₂ft) high dome, its various chapels feature sculptures by Alonso Cano and an El Greco portrait of St Francis.

Of greater interest is its neighbouring Capilla Real, built as a mausoleum for the *reyes católicos*, Isabel and Fernando, as well as their daughter Joana, '*el loco*' (the mad), and her husband Felipe, '*el guapo*' (the handsome). There is, however, doubt whether these are the true remains of Isabel and Fernando, as their original graves in the Alhambra had been defiled before the contents were moved to the Capilla.

Gran Vía de Colón. Cathedral open: Mon–Sat 10am–1.30pm & 4–8pm, Sun 4–8pm. Admission charge. Capilla Real open: Mon–Sat 10.30am–1.30pm & 4–7pm, Sun 11am–1pm & 4–7pm. Admission charge.

Corral del Carbón

An Arab *caravanserai* – inn and warehouse for merchandise – adapted by the Christian *renconqueros* for use as a theatre.
Mariana Pineda. Open: Mon–Fri 10am–1.30pm & 5–8pm, Sat 10.30am–2pm. Free admission.

Plaza Bib-Rambla

A few short blocks from the corner of Gran Via and Reyes Católicos, south of Plaza Nueva, this is the nearest this oddly de-centred city has to a centre. The pretty square is lined with bars and restaurants, handy for the cathedral.

Plaza Nueva

This large space is dominated by the Real Chancelleria, built in the 16th century to house law courts, and the church of Santa Ana. From the top end of the square the Carrera del Darro follows the river of the same name towards the Sacromonte cave and gypsy quarter. Along it or just off it are several important buildings. Behind the Chancelleria, alleys slope steeply up into the Albaicín, but a more comfortable way to get there is to take calle Caldereria Vieja that starts just around the corner from Plaza Nueva, on calle Elvira. From the bottom of the square it is a short distance to the Plaza de Isabel la Católica at the end of the Gran Vía de Colón, Granada's main street.

Nightlife

Here and around Plaza Nueva and the Albaicín are the best places to hunt for a meal, drink or entertainment. The large student population and a lively lesbian/gay community guarantees a plethora of trendy hangouts.

The red fort in winter with the snows of the Sierra Nevada in the distance

More perhaps than any other historic monument in Spain, the Alhambra repays a little pre-planning before a visit. Such is the pressure of tourism on the site that a special system has been set up to process advance ticket applications for the 8,800 visitors allowed in each day. Some 75 per cent of tickets are available through the Banco Bilbao Vizcaya (BBV) by credit card purchase and the rest are sold at the Alhambra itself. Tickets can be purchased by credit card in advance by telephone (*902 22 44 60; from abroad: 00 34 91 557 91 78*) or via the website, *www.alhambratickets.com. For information see www.alhambra-patronato.es*

Access

The Alhambra is reached from Plaza Nueva by car, by the special Alhambra bus service or on foot (*20 mins*) up the

steep wooded Cuesta (hill) de Gomérez. There's a large car park by the entrance, which is to your left.

Planning your visit

The authorities reckon the average visitor needs three hours to visit the Alhambra, which is a conservative estimate. The Alhambra currently opens at 8.30am (ticket office: 8am) and whatever time you decide to visit your ticket will be stamped with a half-hour window (usually an hour or more in advance) during which you must enter the Palacios Nazaries area, although once past the entrance you can stay as long as you like. You should thus plan your route through the Alhambra around this. There are toilets and refreshments (sometimes just vending machines) at various points around the complex, and you should bear in mind that much of the site is out in the open (take hats and sunblock). There is wheelchair access, but not to every nook and cranny, and parts can be very crowded.

History

The oldest parts of the Alhambra, notably the Alcazaba (fortress), date from the 9th century, and later additions up to the 14th century.

The Alhambra takes its name from the Arabic *Al Qal'a al-Hamra* (red fort), from the red-coloured walls of its earliest structures. Little of the earliest

fortress remains, and it was rebuilt in the 11th century and again in the 13th by the Nasrid rulers who were to build the Palacios Nazaries.

The Alcazaba is one of three groups of monuments here, along with the Casas Reales, which include the Palacios, and the adjoining Generalife gardens. At its peak in the 14th century, the Alhambra comprised an entire royal city in miniature.

Ownership changed abruptly after the long winter of 1491–2, when Isabel and Fernando with an army of 150,000 laid siege to this last bastion of Moorish rule, defeating Boabdil in January 1492.

Alcazaba

Much of the original fort is ruined, but some vestiges remain, most notably the **Torre de la Vela** bell tower, named after the bell that used to be rung to mark the hours when the irrigation system watered Granada's Vega, or agricultural plain. The Christian flag was first flown from this battlement on 2 January 1492 to announce the city's capture.

Palacios Nazaries

Across the **Plaza de los Aljibes** (cisterns) is the entry to the Palacios, down a ramp or stairs. This is the area of the Alhambra where you will be allotted a half-hour window to enter – miss it and you'll have to come back another day or buy another ticket. The Palacios are all built around water, light and open spaces. Traffic through them,

Facing page: The Alhambra's masterpiece, the Patio de los Leones
Above: The Palacio del Partal, the oldest remnant of the fort

especially if you get caught between the combat-ready hordes that roam the complex led by their commando-like guides, is slow and one-way.

Mexuar

The first section of the Palacios is a council chamber built around a courtyard in 1365 where the sultan would consult with his viziers and also hear petitions for mercy or favour from his subjects. It leads on through the **Patio del Cuarto Dorado** (Gold Quarter) to the first of the Palacios' marvels, the Serrallo, or harem.

Serrallo

The palace that housed the sultan's wives is approached through the cool rectangular space of the **Patio de Arrayanes**, named after the trimmed

Below: The exquisite Patio de la Acequia in the Generalife gardens

myrtles that hedge its placid pond. As well as the rooms giving on to the arcaded spaces around the pool, this is dominated by the **Salón de Embajadores** (Hall of the Ambassadors), where sensitive matters of state were dealt with and where Boabdil negotiated his surrender in 1492. The Salón has a magnificent latticed wood ceiling, whose criss-crossed knot-like patterns represent the seven heavens of Moorish cosmology.

Harén

The centre of the Serrallo, where the *harén* (harem) occupants would recline, is also the archetypal feature of the Alhambra: the **Patio de los Leones**, with its twelve lions supporting a fountain at the centre of symmetrical watercourses, overlooked by delicate arcading.

The neighbouring **Sala de los Abencerrajes**, named after the family of a rival of Boabdil supposedly slaughtered at a banquet here, has the most impressive ceiling of the entire Alhambra. Its fantastical stucco patterns are based on Pythagoras' famed theorem about the properties of the right-angled triangle.

Palacio de Carlos V

The exit from the Palacios leads into this later, Christian addition to the complex, built in the 16th century by the eponymous king. This Renaissance palace was never finished, but now serves as the **Museo Hispano-Musulman** (*open: Tue–Sat 9.30am–2pm; admission charge, EU citizens free*) which has an excellent collection of Spanish–Moorish artefacts.

Generalife

The neighbouring gardens, translated variously from the Arabic *Yannat al Arif* as 'gardens of the architect' or 'lofty paradise', were begun in the 13th century and originally included orchards and pasture. Later designs transformed them into a maze of exquisite watercourses and topiary ideal for romantic intrigues.

Alhambra and Generalife (*open: Mar–Oct 8.30am–10pm, Nov–Feb 8.30am–6pm; admission charge*).

Convento de San Francisco

Behind the *palacio* are the remains of the original royal city, including its convent, nowadays serving as Granada's over-priced *parador* hotel, which is often booked up months in advance. The bar and restaurant are open to non-residents, and the garden is a great place to drink in the view.

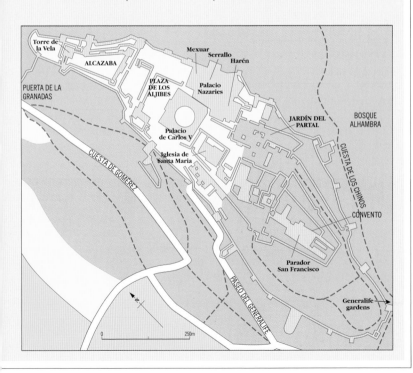

Walk: the Albaicín

The hill opposite the Alhambra is occupied by the Albaicín, the most perfectly preserved Moorish quarter in Andalucía. Most of the streets are narrow and stepped, meaning that you'll meet few cars to bother you. The characteristic house of the Albaicín is the *carmen*, a villa concealed behind high walls. You can get up to the viewpoint at the top of the Albaicín and back in an hour, but for a leisurely stroll allow two hours.

1 Plaza Nueva

The walk begins in this busy square, on a corner of which, beside the church of Santa Ana, stands the tourist office. Plaza Nueva is dominated by the Real Chancelleria, the Royal Chancellery, designed by Diego de Siloé and completed in 1530.

2 Placeta de San Miguel Bajo

Take Carcel Alta, the street to the left of the Chancellery as you look at it. Turn left at the top and turn sharp right in the cobbled square of Plaza San Gregorio. Almost immediately turn off left heading steeply uphill on the short Grifos de San José. Bear left at the end and right when you meet Placeta de San José. Ahead of you is the lovely 10th-century minaret of San José. Go uphill underneath this, passing the handsome doorway of the Carmen San Luis. Turn right and quick left to cross calle Bocanegra and continue uphill into Placeta de San Miguel Bajo, dominated by a whitewashed church. Note the Moorish cistern in the corner of the square.

The Real Chancelleria, built for the *reyes católicos* by master architect Diego de Siloé

slopes, there is also an astronomy programme and there are hiking routes around the resort.

There are three daily buses from Granada to Pradollano (four at weekends), leaving from one of the stops on the roundabout by the Palacio de Congresos (over the Rio Genil from central Granada). There is also a twice-daily out-of-season service, as well as possible alternatives from the main bus station on the western limits of the city, situated near the *circunvalación* (bypass). *For further information, tel: 902 70 80 90; www.sierranevada.es*

Thousands of *granadinos* take to the slopes on winter weekends

Walk: Sierra Nevada/ Pradollano

This is a short mountain walk for the summer months, and with optional detours or cut-offs along the way. It is circular, with an average round-trip time of five hours, less if you opt for some of the swifter return routes. It shifts between paths, tracks and roads. At this altitude (above 2,000m/6,562ft, rising to over 3,000m/9,842ft) the usual warnings about wearing firm footwear and protective clothing and taking adequate supplies and sunburn precautions need to be stressed.

A shorter winter option still is to make the walk circular but with Estación de Borreguiles as the destination, either by taking the road and path up and the ski lift down, or vice versa.

The walk can be begun either from Pradollano, which has public transport connections, or in the vicinity of the

Heading up above the snow line

Albergue Universitario, the youth hostel used by students from Granada and elsewhere during study trips.

1 Pradollano
There are two options from Pradollano to Borreguiles, either the conventional walk described below or a quicker cheat's walk using the ski lift (not operating in summer). The second route is also an option if you just want to walk part of the way, say to the astronomical observatory, and turn back.

2 Albergue Universitario
If you decide to walk, take the A-395 mountain road from Pradollano up to the Albergue. Here take the path signposted off to the right heading for the Virgen de las Nieves area, one of the numerous parascending (*parapente*)

spots here. This leads to the Cruce (crossroads) de Borreguiles, where the path forks left and right, the former following the road on up.

3 Borreguiles
The right-hand path strikes off into open country and towards the Estación de Borreguiles ski-lift station. Above the station to the west (left) is the IRAM radio telescope station, one of three observatories this route passes.

4 Embalse de las Yeguas
From Borreguiles, the route continues up in a fairly straightforward fashion until reaching the second observatory, above a T-junction where another path joins this route from the west (your right). Continue straight on until you reach the Embalse de las Yeguas, a small lake-like reservoir, and a series of smaller lakelets beyond.
Here another T-junction leads left and right: take the left fork, heading back towards the road at Carihuela.

5 Carihuela
At Carihuela, there are various options. You are within striking distance of the peak of El Veleta, second only in height to its neighbour, Mulhacen, Spain's highest peak. Several other high-ridge walks leave here, including a circular route via Garro del Caballo, and an even longer march over the peaks to Capileira (*see pp106–7*). However, these are beyond the reach of the day walker, and anyone without serious gear and experience.
The simplest route back to Pradollano or the Albergue is by the (blocked) road as it zigzags back down, or the quicker but rougher route as the track cuts across the meanders of the road down to Cruce de Borreguiles. The path continues to shortcut across the road's turns, passing under the third observatory seen on this route, down to the Albergue.

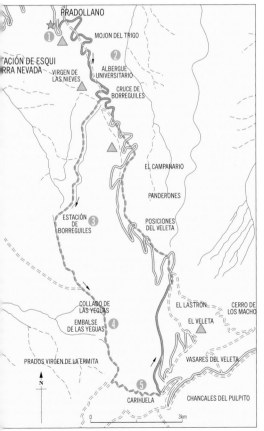

PRADOLLANO
MOJON DEL TRIGO
ESTACIÓN DE ESQUI
SIERRA NEVADA
VIRGEN DE LAS NIEVES
ALBERGUE UNIVERSITARIO
CRUCE DE BORREGUILES
EL CAMPANARIO
PANDERONES
ESTACIÓN DE BORREGUILES
POSICIONES DEL VELETA
COLLADO DE LAS YEGUAS
EL LASTRÓN
CERRO DE LOS MACHO
EMBALSE DE LAS YEGUAS
EL VELETA
PRADOS VIRGEN DE LA ERMITA
VASARES DEL VELETA
N
CARIHUELA
CHANCALES DEL PULPITO
0   3km

Jaén

Probably the least prepossessing city in Andalucía, Jaén nevertheless has a number of attractions worth a detour and makes an excellent base or overnight stop for exploring the region. Its Santa Catalina castle (best viewed at twilight arriving from Granada) has one of the most dramatic sites in the whole of Spain.

The Baños Árabes

A centre of olive production since Roman times and earlier (archaeological finds have established links with Greek sea traders), Jaén city and province have been dominated, geographically and economically, by the doughty *olea Europea* (European olive) for millennia. A key post in Moorish *al-Andalus*, it was recaptured by Fernando III's armies in 1246 and entered an economic decline that only saw an upswing in the past century.

Next to the spectacular castle (**Castillo de Santa Catalina**; *open: Tue–Sun 10am–2pm & 5–9pm; admission charge*) is now a draughty and campily mock-baronial *parador* (*bar/restaurant open to non-guests*) and at 5km (3 miles) by road and an hour on foot is best experienced at a distance. In the town, however, particularly in the *casco antiguo* behind the monumental cathedral, there are some fascinating sights. Jaén is also a university town, with a separate art school, and a student culture to match.

Catedral

The cathedral itself dwarfs the town almost as much as the Catalina castle – its twin towers are over 60m (196ft) high. Tinkered with by a variety of architects over the centuries, including Andrés de Vandelvira, it's a masterpiece of Renaissance architecture. The cathedral museum holds some important religious artefacts collected from around the region.
Catedral, Plaza de la Constitucíon/Santa María. Open: Mon–Sat 8.30am–1pm & 5–8pm, Sun 9am–1pm & 6–8pm. Free admission.

Baños Árabes

Probably the most important site after the castle and cathedral is the Arab baths, which are among the finest preserved examples in Spain, and is in fact just one of three museums now housed in a 16th-century palace that was deliberately built over the remains.

The baths themselves were built on what were probably the remains of earlier Roman baths, taking advantage of hot water springs that suggest volcanic activity in the region. A glass floor has been placed over the central sections so that visitors walk over the remains as though through the air.

Above the baths, on the ground floor and upper levels of the 16th-century **Palacio de Villadompardo**, is the **Ethnological Museum**, dedicated to the olive industry and domestic customs over the centuries. The Ethnological Museum shares its upper floor with the curious **Museo Internacional de Arte Naif**, a collection of largely Spanish naïve art. A lower gallery is also dedicated to contemporary art works.
Baños Árabes, calle Martínez Molina. Open: Tue–Fri 9am–8pm, Sat–Sun 9.30am–2.30pm. Free admission.

Museo Provincial
This small museum dedicated to local history is also worth a visit for its fascinating collection of Iberian sculptures dating from around the 5th century BC and displaying a marked Greek influence, further suggesting an early Greek presence in this olive-dependent region.
Paseo de la Estación. Open: Tue 2.30–8.30pm, Wed–Sat 9am–8.30pm, Sun 9am–2.30pm. Free admission.

Jaén's mountainous cathedral looming above the old town

Parque Natural de Cazorla

The peaks, slopes and thickly wooded valleys of the Parque Natural de Cazorla, Segura y las Villas were once the preferred shooting fiefdom of Franco and his cronies. Now they have been gathered together as Spain's largest nature reserve, taking up almost a fifth of the area of Jaén province. There are still game hunters at large, but little disturbs the peace of this beautiful corner of Andalucía.

Cazorla and its castles

Cazorla

Clinging to the mountainside in the sierra of the same name, the town of Cazorla could almost be alpine with a jumble of gable-roofed houses and steep streets and alleys. It serves as an information office and service centre for the nature reserve, with a wide choice of accommodation and reasonably good transport links. It is a place of some history, having Roman remains and two Moorish castles, one in the town and one just outside it (La Yedra), which contains a folk museum. Another interesting monument is the ruined 16th-century church, the Iglesia de Santa María, which was razed by Napoleon's troops in the Peninsular War.

Several companies based in Cazorla offer guided walks and outdoor activities in the reserve, including Quercus and TierraAventura.
Excursiones Quercus, calle Juan Domingo 2. Tel: 953 72 01 15.
TierraAventura Cazorla, calle Ximénez de Rada 17. Tel: 953 72 20 11.

The road through the reserve

A single main road leads from Cazorla under the castle of La Iruela and over the Puerto de las Palomas, before descending to a crossroads, the Empalme del Valle. Most visitors turn northeast up the valley from here, but the *parador* (part of a chain of luxury, state-run hotels) makes an interesting visit, not for the building itself, which is modern, but for its beautiful location. A long detour from the crossroads (return trip of about 40km/25 miles) leads to the source of the Guadalquivir River.

The road down the valley brings you instead to the Torre del Vinagre visitors' centre, which has a botanic garden next to it. There is also a hunting museum and, not far away, a fish farm. Deer and mouflon can be seen living in semi-liberty in the game park of **Parque Cinegético del Collado del Almendral**.

From the visitors' centre a scenic route runs beside an elongated reservoir, the Embalse del Tranco, towards more open country at the north of the nature reserve. A left turning through the gorge of the upper Guadalquivir returns you to the olive-growing hills and plains of Jaén at Iznatoraf.

Segura de la Sierra

In the far north of the nature reserve is this town, which was important in Moorish times as testified by its Arab baths and walls. Its magnificent castle – visible long before you get near the town – was built in the 13th and 14th centuries when Segura was ruled by the Knights of Santiago. There are impressive views from the top of the *torre de homenaje* (keep). The peak of **El Yelmo** at 1,805m (5,922ft) is popular among hang-gliders. Nearby Hornos is another hill town dominated by a castle.

The ruins of the Iglesia de Santa María at the centre of Cazorla

Walk: Quesada and Tiscar

In both summer and winter, the mountain routes above Cazorla offer some of the most spectacular views in the whole of Andalucía. This route, largely on roads, involves some improvisation with transport, or some serious hiking, but the vistas are worth it. There are numerous off-road routes around Cazorla, best taken with the guidance of one of the travel companies in the town, but they require at least a two-day stay in Cazorla.

This route can be completed in half a day, although you might want to factor a local taxi ride into part(s) of the route. Allow about 4 hours.

1 Quesada

The route begins in the village of Quesada, although you could conceivably join it by taking the mountain road opposite the petrol station on the A-319 Úbeda road just outside Cazorla.

Olive groves between Cazorla and Quesada

Quesada itself is a small mountain village with little tourism, although it has an intriguing museum to local painter Rafael Zabaleta, who reappears later on this route.

2 Puerto de Tiscar

The road south towards Tiscar rises into the mountains below spectacular cliffs to the east (your right). Views in the opposite direction are out over the Sierra de Cazorla and the sea of olive groves below, and just get better and better. The little-used road (a particular favourite of locals) winds up through pines to the plateau of the Puerto de Tiscar, the Tiscar Pass. At 1,800m (5,905ft), this is only 200m (656ft) below the peak of Cabañas, the elephantine mountain looming over Cazorla. Views back, and, shortly, forwards, are stunning, perfected only if you climb up to the Moorish *atalaya* (watchtower), a short clamber up from the road.

3 Tiscar

From here the road begins to wind down towards the hamlet of Tiscar, below increasingly dramatic rock cliffs and overhangs, and, as often as not, raptors circling on thermals. As Tiscar comes into view below, so does a distinctly architectural shape in the jagged rock formations silhouetted above it. This is the Santuario de Tiscar, a Moorish fort built on a dizzying perch above the gorge carrying the Rio Quesada. The fort was captured by the Christians in the early 14th century and turned into a shrine to the Virgin Mary. Today it boasts a painting by Zabaleta recording Quesada's annual *romeria* (religious procession) to the Virgin here. *There are a number of restaurants here, overlooking the river, where you might stop for lunch or arrange for a Cazorla taxi to collect you.*

4 Huesa or Cabañas

A right-hand turning just beyond Tiscar leads down to Huesa and a lower route returning to Quesada. Alternatively, the same road on from Tiscar continues up on to the flank of Cabañas, past an extensive fire-damaged area of forest, and to a turning off that will lead, at some distance, to the source of the Guadalquivir, a journey only really viable by four-wheel drive.

5 Nacimiento del Rio Guadalquivir

Instead of taking the Huesa turning, you can make a much longer walk by continuing in the direction of Pozo Alcon from Tiscar and taking the left turn under the peaks of Palomas and Cabañas to reach the Nacimiento del Rio Guadalquivir. From here you can either go over Puerto Larente to Cazorla, or walk down the Guadalquivir valley to join the main road through the nature reserve beyond Puente de las Herrerias.

Úbeda and Baeza

Úbeda and Baeza are two Renaissance gems: old town centres composed of handsome palaces and churches, which were built between the 15th and 17th centuries when riches flowed into the region. None of the monuments here is of singular interest: it is the harmony of the whole which is so attractive – the pleasing streets and squares, and the details you come across. Both these towns are great places to stroll around at leisure.

Úbeda's Plaza Vázquez de Molina

Both Úbeda and Baeza trace their histories back to the Roman presence, but the towns we see today were created after the Reconquest, when both fell to the Christians within a short time of each other in the 13th century. Each was built by the newly landed gentry created by the *reyes católicos*, although this process was not without its tensions. Inter-clan rivalries in Úbeda grew so fierce that the royal family had the town walls demolished so that the army could intervene in the battles raging between its dynasties (after whom most of the streets are named).

Baeza

Baeza too had its awkward customers: Isabel ordered that its Alcázar be torn down because sparring families kept using it as a redoubt in their violent squabbles. The Renaissance marvels that remain intact are a short stroll from the central Plaza de España and Paseo de la Constitución. Just off the southern tip of España is Baeza's most striking Renaissance palace, the **Palacio de Jabalquinto**, and next to it the **Antigua**

Universidad (Old University). Nearby is the town's cathedral, **Catedral de Santa María**, with a nave by Vandelvira.
Palacio de Jabalquinto, calle Romanones (patio only). Open: Mon–Fri 9am–2pm. Free admission.
Catedral de Santa María, Plaza de Santa María. Open: daily 10.30am–1pm & 5–9pm. Free admission.

Ayuntamiento

Originally the town court and prison, this remarkable building of 1559 sits a block from Paseo de la Constitución on calle Benavides; parts of it are open to the public. On the corner is the (private) house occupied by a former Antigua Universidad employee, the poet Antonio Machado, who also has a *paseo* named after him on the eastern edge of the town. The greatest concentration of Renaissance palaces is north of here.
Ayuntamiento, calle Benavides. Tel: 953 74 01 54. Open: by arrangement only.

Úbeda

The old centre of Úbeda is so postcard-perfect it could be a film set. Between

Plaza de Andalucía and the southerly town walls near Puerta de Granada, magnificent palaces and mansions jostle for attention along its cobbled streets and squares. At its heart sits the Plaza Vázquez de Molina, named after one of the aforementioned feuding families. This one square boasts no fewer than five buildings by Renaissance master Andrés de Vandelvira. On the west side is the **Palacio de las Cadenas**, which now houses the *ayuntamiento*. At its eastern end is the Gothic church of **Santa María de los Reales Alcázares**, the neighbouring **Carcel del Obispo**, and across from this the **Palacio de Marqués de Mancera**, which faces the **Palacio del Condestable Dávalos**, nowadays Úbeda's *parador*. There are more Vandelvira buildings to be found in the neighbouring Plaza del Primero de Mayo and nearby streets. The remaining city walls encircling the *casco antiguo* can be circumnavigated in under an hour.

There is only one important building not in the city centre – also by Vandelvira (in fact considered his best and most mature work). The **Hospital de Santiago** was built as a poor hospital, and now stands stranded in the outskirts near the bullring. It has a sombre but decorated façade, and a monumental staircase.

Ornate stone carving in Baeza

Córdoba

Córdoba is one of the three great cities of Andalucía, along with Seville and Granada. Unique among European cities it focuses on a mosque, one of immense historical and architectural significance, and it is this that most visitors come to see. But Córdoba's reputation rests on much more than that: it also has a castle, palaces, several good museums and above all a warren of medieval streets and leafy patios to explore.

The Mezquita interior

History

Archaeologists have tracked agricultural settlements here back to the neolithic period (4000–2000 BC) and have found evidence of trade – possibly seaborne, with olive-tree-bearing Greeks – dating back to the second millennium BC. Córdoba, or Corduba as it was named, became an important city under Roman rule in the 2nd century BC, and from 152 BC was the capital of Rome's Hispania Ulterior, the northernmost region of Baetica (Roman Spain) and roughly the size and shape of Andalucía. The city prospered on agriculture and mining, and produced the poets Lucan (AD 39–65) and Seneca (AD 4–65), tutor and ill-fated mentor to Nero.

With Roman influence in decline, Córdoba – like the rest of the Iberian peninsula – fell prey to Visigoth and Vandal insurgence. The city was taken by the Moors in 711, the same year that Tariq ibn Ziyad landed at Gibraltar. In 756 it was declared the capital of Moorish Spain, under Abd ar-Rahman, who proclaimed himself the emir, independent ruler, of al-Andalus, and head of the

Omayyad dynasty. Ar-Rahman oversaw the building of la Mezquita between 785 and 787 – later rulers would expand and alter it (*see pp142–3*).

By 929, with Abd ar-Rahman III now self-declared caliph and wholly independent of Baghdad, Córdoba was the largest city in Europe. In effect, the concentration of knowledge, culture and power made Córdoba the centre of the western world. This high-water mark in the city's history would produce such thinkers as Averroës and Maimonides (*see pp12–13*).

The Omayyad dynasty was torn apart in the 11th century by internecine battles between rival Berber tribes and insurgent Christian Reconquista armies from the north. Córdoba slipped into the shadow of Seville, and finally fell to the Christians in 1236. It then entered a period of economic and political decline that was only reversed in the latter half of the 20th century.

The modern city

Córdoba is a compact and walkable city, with its *casco antiguo* centred, naturally, on la Mezquita, and the later, post-Reconquest city built around and east of the central Plaza de las Tendillas. The city centre is shaped by the curving Rio Guadalquivir as it passes the easterly limits of the old town.

While la Mezquita is a tourist honeytrap, perhaps unfortunately so given the level of vulgar commercialisation clustered around its walls, there is much more to Córdoba, as can be found on an easy stroll around the old town (*see pp144–5*).

Alcázar de los Reyes Cristianos
Alfonso XI had this fortress built in 1368, and it was used by Isabel and Fernando during their campaign to conquer Granada. It was later used by the Inquisition and, later still, as a prison, until the mid-20th century. The depredations of time have erased much of the earlier detail, but it retains beautiful mosaics and other artefacts in the interior, and landscaped gardens and waterways in the grounds.
Calle Caballerizas Reales. Tel: 957 42 01 51. Open: Tue–Sat 10am–2pm & 5.30–7.30pm, Sun 9.30am–2.30pm. Admission charge but free on Fri.

Museo Arqueológico
As befits a city groaning with so much history, Córdoba's archaeological

Watercourses and landscaped gardens in the interior of Córdoba's Alcázar

museum offers an excellent introduction to its prehistoric, Roman and Moorish past. The 16th-century mansion housing the museum, Casa Páez, contains an authentic Roman mosaic discovered during renovation work.
Plaza de Jerónimo Páez. Open: Tue 2.30–8.30pm, Wed–Sat 9am–8.30pm, Sun 9am–2.30pm. Admission charge (EU citizens free).

Museo de Bellas Artes and Palacio de Viana

While many of its paintings were siphoned off to the Prado, the Museo still contains works by Murillo, Leal and

Monument to Maimonides in Córdoba

Zurburán. The Palacio de Viana is a museum dedicated to the Viana family, who began the palace in the 14th century and whose heirs sold it in the 1980s. The guided tour is forgettable, but the palace has no fewer than a dozen superb patios.
Museo de Bellas Artes, Plaza del Potro. Open: Tue 2.30–8.30pm, Wed–Sat 9am–8.30pm, Sun 9am–2.30pm. Admission charge (EU citizens free). Palacio de Viana, Plaza de Gome. Open: Mon–Sat 10am–1pm & 4–6pm. Admission charge.

Córdoba's plazas

Córdoba's past and present meet in its squares and plazas. Plaza del Potro was once a livestock market and the area maintained a fairly rough reputation for centuries. Renovated, it is home to the **Posada del Potro**, named in *Don Quixote* and nowadays a contemporary art gallery. Plaza de las Tendillas is the centre of the modern city, but this is also the area where you will find many of Córdoba's historic churches, which are usually locked outside service hours and best visited around early evening.
Posada del Potro. Open: daily 9.30am–2.30pm & 4.30–7pm.

Medina Azahara

As well as declaring himself caliph, Abd ar-Rahman III also built an entirely new capital 7km (4 miles) west of the city. At its peak, Medina Azahara was an ambitious creation: one hall prefigured holographics by employing crystals to create man-made rainbows, while another used a vast pan of mercury tilted by a slave to produce lightning effects to impress the caliph's visitors. For 30 years until its perhaps inevitable destruction, ar-Rahman dedicated a third of the caliphate's annual wealth to this bizarre indulgence, named after a favourite wife, az-Zahra. Abd ar-Rahman was eventually sidelined by one of his viziers, Ibn Abi Amir, later known as Al-Mansur (the victor), but Amir's attempts to construct his own caliphate were thwarted by civil war among various factions. Medina Azahara was razed by Berber mercenaries, and only rediscovered at the beginning of the 20th century. Barely a fraction of the site has been uncovered, but a series of vestigial structures can be seen while excavations continue.

Open: Tue–Sat 10am–8.30pm, Sun 10am–2pm. Admission charge (EU citizens free).

A colourful courtyard in Córdoba

Córdoba province

Most visitors to Córdoba tend to concentrate their time in the capital – with, perhaps, a foray to Medina Azahara – and they leave with barely a glance at the province around it. Although this extends from vast, monotonous olive groves in the south to the desolate slopes of the Sierra Morena in the north, it includes some sights worth the effort of getting to, including Spain's 'alternative' sherry centre, a handsome baroque town and an enchanting mini-mountain range with its own white towns.

Fernán Nuñez

Almodovar del Río

Although built originally by the Arabs in 760, this magnificent castle above a town on the Guadalquivir River, 17km (11 miles) downstream from Córdoba, is largely a reconstruction. It plays on a faux historical theme offering visitors all things medieval: a gift shop, banquets, markets and a programme of cultural events on the same theme.
Open: Mon–Fri 11am–2.30pm & 4–7pm, Sat 11am–7pm. Admission charge.

Priego de Córdoba

Córdoba province's finest town was filled with baroque architecture during the 17th and 18th centuries on the proceeds of the silk and textile industry. The chief sight is a fountain, La Fuente del Rey, consisting of three ornamental basins fed by 139 spouts. Priego also has a pretty Moorish quarter to explore, the Barrio de la Villa.

Sierra Subbética

It may not be as famous or as much visited as some of Andalucía's other mountain ranges, but the Sierra Subbetica has its share of attractive scenery and interesting villages. The best place to stay overnight is **Zuheros**, a cluster of winding streets of brilliant white houses beneath a castle. Above the town is the **Cueva de los Murcielagos**, a 2km (1¼-mile) long cave decorated with Stone Age paintings, of which 450m (1,476ft) with 700 steps is open to the public.

Two towns on the edge of the sierra worth dipping into are **Baena**, famed for its olive oil, and **Cabra**, which has several old churches and aristocratic mansions.
Cueva de los Murcielagos open: 12.30–5.30pm (closes at 4.30pm in winter). Admission charge.

Montilla

Jerez de la Frontera (*see pp52–3*) may get all the fame with its sherry, but Córdoba's equivalent town of Montilla claims its wines are just as good without any need to fortify them. Still, at least it gets remembered in the name Amontillado – the term for pale, dry sherry. Several of the wine producers (*bodegas*) will give you a tour. The largest is Alvear, which also claims to be the oldest bodega in Spain.

At the opposite end of town from Bodegas Alvear are the Mudéjar-style convent of Santa Clara with a carved portal, and the so-called Casa del Inca, the former home of Garcilaso de la Vega, Spain's historian of the Incas.

Aguilar, a short way south of Montilla, has a grand 19th-century octagonal main square. **Fernán Nuñez**, to the north, on the way to Córdoba city, is dominated by the palace of the Dukes of Fernán Nuñez, built in the 1780s, with a restored formal terraced garden behind it.

Bodegas Alvear, Avenida María Auxiliadora. Tel: 957 65 01 00. Open: Mon–Fri 10am–2pm, Sat 11am–2pm. Reserve your visit in advance if possible. Admission charge.

Old building in Baena

Córdoba's Mezquita (mosque) is unique in Europe: an (almost) intact 10th-century Moorish place of worship, a stunning example of Moorish architecture. Parts were later destroyed (although some time after the Reconquest) to allow the construction of a Christian cathedral, but not even this act of desecration can reduce the effect of the archwork or the exquisite *mihrab* (prayer niche).

Construction

The Mezquita actually dates from a variety of eras, incorporating various architectural styles and materials from Visigothic and even Roman times. The building we see today was built in four distinct stages (five if we include the cathedral). The first stage, inwards from the Puerta de San Esteban and including the Patio de los Naranjos, was built in 785 by Abd ar-Rahman I on the site of a Visigothic church, although much of his original design disappeared under the 16th-century cathedral. As would be the case elsewhere in the mosque, his architect Sidi ben Ayub incorporated materials, including the exterior wall, from an earlier Visigothic cathedral that had stood on the site.

Ayub's design was extended by Rahman I's successor Abd ar-Rahman II and again in the 10th century by Al-Hakam II, who added the grand ornamented *mihrab*. The oblong shape seen today was completed in the last years of the 10th century by Al-Mansur. His chief contribution was to extend the prayer hall to something the size of a football pitch, with an arched roof requiring 850 columns of granite, jasper and marble. Again, a great deal of this material was taken from earlier structures, including Visigothic and Roman places of worship. As the mosque could not be extended further to the south because of the river, Al-Mansur extended it east. The Moorish arches, themselves an improvisation on an earlier Visigothic arch pattern, used alternating brick and stone to achieve the red and white motif, an innovation in Moorish architecture. At its finest, the mosque was the second largest in the world and it is said that up to 40,000 people could pray in it at any one time.

Catedral

The cathedral at the heart of the mosque wasn't in fact begun until 1523, following three centuries of relatively minor tinkering with the original structure. The first Christian edifice to be built within the mosque was the Capilla de Villaviciosa, built by Moorish craftsmen in 1371, followed by the Mudéjar-style Puerta del Perdón. The most serious effect of this was to wall in the prayer hall that had previously been open to the Patio de los Naranjos, where the faithful had prepared for prayer. What had been a light and airy place of worship became a dark and gloomy place of atonement.

Curiously, given the history of post-Reconquest Spain, the Córdoban authorities exercised considerable restraint in their handling of the building. It would seem that the chapter, or religious authorities, of the chapel wanted to impose a Christian edifice on the Mezquita, and in 1523 King Carlos I overruled the advice of the Córdobans and authorised the project. Famously, Carlos regretted the result of his decision, telling the cathedral architects 'You have destroyed something that was unique in the world.'

La Mezquita. Calle Torrijos 10. Tel: 957 47 05 12. Open: daily 10am–7pm, although times can vary month by month. Admission charge.

The Mezquita at Córdoba is probably the most exquisite Muslim monument in the West

Walk: Moorish Córdoba

Córdoba's old town is a particularly beautiful place for a stroll, especially during the first week of May, when the city celebrates its Festival de los Patios, in which the inhabitants of the older houses decorate their patios with plants, pots, mirrors and water features.

This short walk can be completed in under an hour. If you are visiting for the day by bus or train you can enter the old town via the Puerta de Almodóvar at the bottom of the Jardines de la Victoria and begin the walk there.

Commercialisation is fairly intense in the streets immediately around la Mezquita, although at least you can find a drink or meal here. There are also shops and bars spread around the quieter areas away from the mosque.

1 Torre de Calahorra

The walk begins across the river at the Torre de Calahorra. Although it was

The Mezquita tower

built after Córdoba fell to the Christians, nowadays the tower contains a small museum dedicated to Córdoba's Moorish history and a rather portentous homily on the family of man.
Open: 10am–2pm & 4.30–8.30pm (6pm in winter). Admission charge.

2 Calle de Torrijos

Cross the Puente Romano (the Moorish waterwheel on your left is a reconstruction), pausing briefly by the Puerta del Puente gate to admire the city's patron saint, San Rafael, atop his 18th-century monument. Straight ahead is calle de Torrijos, flanked on the right by the **Mezquita** (*see pp142–3*) and on the left by the Palacio Episcopal (closed for restoration). There is also a tourist information office near here.

3 Cardenal Herrero

Turn left by the Torre del Alminar, the site of la Mezquita's original minaret, on to Cardenal Herrero, where the modern *parador* is built on the site of a Moorish palace. At the end of Herrero, walk round to calle Blanco, which gives on to a number of *callejóns* (alleys), including the famous Callejón de las Flores, whose walls and courtyards erupt with flowers in spring and especially during the Festival de los Patios.

4 Plaza Maimonides and Judería

From calle Blanco, take Luque to calle Deanes, right on calle Romero then left up to Plaza Maimonides, where a statue of the great Moorish philosopher marks the site of his home. Here also is the small Museo Taurino (Bullfighting Museum; closed for restoration) that celebrates, among others, Córdoban legend Manolete – not to mention Islero, the bull who gored Manolete to death during a *corrida* at Linares in 1947 and whose hide is displayed beside a replica of the matador's tomb. This is the heart

of the Judería, the old Jewish quarter, and the site of the former **Sinagoga** (*open: Tue–Sat 9.30am–2pm & 3.30–5.30pm, Sun 9.30am–1.30pm; admission charge, EU citizens free*), with some fascinating Hebrew texts fashioned in Mudéjar style. This is one of just three remaining synagogues left since the Jews were driven out of Spain after the Reconquest.

5 Calle Fernández Ruano and Puerta de Almodóvar

Just beyond the synagogue, calle de Cairuan and Calle Fernández Ruano will take you to the Puerta de Almodóvar, convenient if you're heading back to the train or bus station. Otherwise avenida Doctor Fleming leads down to Plaza Campo de los Martires, where there is a ruined Moorish *hammam* (bath) and the Alcázar. Beyond this is the river.

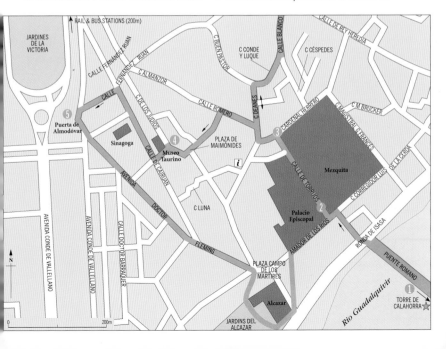

The term 'Reconquest' is a misnomer, but so in this context are the words 'Spain' and 'Moor'. Prior to Tariq ibn Ziyad's invasion of AD 711, there was no unified 'Spain' to be reconquered, rather a ragbag of small kingdoms jockeying for power, at odds with their neighbours and often found in cahoots with parts of what would later become 'France', 'Holland' or 'Germany'. Similarly, 'Moor' is a particularly wide brush used to paint numerous North African cultures.

The Reconquest was an ideological battle, as the gusto with which Isabel and Fernando pursued their agenda suggests. Having ejected the barbarians, the *reyes católicos* set about expelling Protestants, Jews, Morisco 'converts' and anyone else who disagreed with them. In modern terms, the Reconquest might be seen more as the ethnic cleansing of various peoples who had lived in Andalucía for centuries. It was also a battle to reassert vested interests: a tiny aristocratic elite became immensely wealthy by appropriating al-Andalus and the rest of Moorish Spain from the Moors.

This noted, we should also reconsider the 'Moors'. Recent decades have seen historians turning against the 'Eurocentric' reading of the Reconquest that sided with the armies of God against the armies of Mohammed. As any visitor to Seville, Granada or Córdoba will see, the Moors brought great learning to al-Andalus. A journey

through modern Andalucía will also show what their water technologies did to the near deserts here. Yet the successive waves of North African invaders were just as bellicose as their opponents, and capable of equal cruelty. The fact that it took one 'side' 709 years to win and the other 709 years to lose is surely a measure of the ferocity of the armies on both sides.

The element of surprise

The real surprise was the ease with which the Berbers took the southwesternmost tip of Spain, sweeping north and meeting their first real resistance at Jerez in AD 712, where they defeated King Rodrigo and his army and effectively took control of Spain.

The Reconquest is commonly taken to have begun in AD 722 with the semi-legendary Christian victory at Covadonga in Asturias, one of the few regions not to have been overrun by the Moors.

For the next few hundred years or so, battlelines rippled back and forth across the Iberian landscape, frequently depositing the suffix 'de la Frontera' (of the frontier) on spots on the map where the Christians established a foothold. The turning point came, finally, with the Christian victory at Las Navas de Tolosa, in northern Jaén, in 1212. Yet it would be another 280 years before the final Moorish stronghold, Granada, fell.

It used to be said that there were houses in Cairo, Tangier and elsewhere with the keys to houses in Granada, Ronda and other Andalucían cities still hung over the mantelpiece, waiting for their rightful owners to reclaim them from the infidels. They are, of course, already here: in the gene pool, in the architecture and, rather tellingly, in the name.

Facing page: Waterwheels used to irrigate the Alcázar gardens at Córdoba
Below: Los reyes católicos, Ferdinand and Isabel, give Columbus his orders

Getting away from it all

From the deserted beaches of the Costa de la Luz to the ski slopes of the Sierra Nevada, and from the dune systems of Almería to the primordial forests of the Sierra de Grazalema, Andalucía boasts a variety of landscapes unrivalled in the rest of Spain. With a car or timetables for trains and buses, almost all of them are within easy reach of even the largest cities.

The only way to fly

A hire car will enable you to cross Andalucía in half a day. Public transport, however, is a good alternative, and one that will allow you to concentrate on the landscape, and people, rather than the road in front of you. It's clean, safe and efficient. It can also be surprisingly cheap: a bus journey of a few hours or a hundred or more kilometres might cost just a handful of euros.

All but the smallest villages are served by competing private bus companies, some of which – Alsina Graells, Lara, Portillo – have routes that cover most of Andalucía and beyond. There are also frequent connections for destinations such as Madrid and Barcelona and destinations outside Spain as well.

Spain's excellent nationalised rail system RENFE (Red Naciónal de Ferrocarriles Españoles, National Network of Spanish Trains) has a comprehensive inter-city network, which links many of the smaller towns and villages, but little in the way of suburban services (the Málaga–Fuengirola line and Jerez–Sevilla being handy exceptions). Many services cross at the middle-of-nowhere junction of Bobadilla, equidistant between Seville and Granada, and the *enlace* (change) for trains to Málaga and Algeciras. The Ronda–Algeciras route is often listed as one of the most spectacular train rides in Europe. There are also fast links with Madrid and a daily overnight Trenhotel between Málaga and Barcelona. RENFE has a website in Spanish and English (*www.renfe.es*).

Andalucía also has its own modest answer to the Orient Express, the Al-Andalus Expreso. Using stylishly renovated antique rolling stock, it offers six-day itineraries around the region starting from either Seville or Madrid (*tel: 917 88 83 15; www.alandalusexpreso.com*).

Morocco

Most of the coast between Málaga and Tarifa, and inland as far as Gaucín, has views of Africa floating on its southern horizon. Algeciras, Gibraltar and Tarifa have the quickest connections to ports such as Tangier, with over 20 different ferry and catamaran services a day: most Costa del Sol resorts and towns in western Andalucía will have agencies offering day trips and longer stopovers.

Both Málaga and Almería have connections with the Spanish enclaves of Ceuta and Melilla, but at six and seven hours one way this is more an extended trip and neither has the attractions of Tangier.

The largest operator of services to North Africa is Acciona Trasmediterránea, with regular services from Algeciras to Tangier and Almería to Nador and Ghazaouet.
Acciona Trasmediterránea. Tel: 902 45 46 45; www.trasmediterranea.es

Outdoor pursuits

Andalucía's remoter regions, notably the Alpujarras, the Serranía de Ronda and the natural parks of Cazorla and Segura, all offer a variety of outdoor activities, such as hiking, horse riding, mountain biking, canoeing, caving, climbing, canyoning, parascending (*parapente*), hang-gliding and even ballooning. Hotels and local tourist offices stock leaflets about these. A number of companies also offer painting holidays in Andalucía, while others specialise in subjects including cuisine, ornithology and astronomy. Below is a selection of some of these.

Astronomy
Salitre Hotel and Observatorio Astronómico
Algatocín, Málaga; tel: 952 11 70 05; www.turismosalitre.com

Hotel-campsite in the Serranía de Ronda with its own observatory and 9cm (3$^{1}/_{2}$in) reflector telescope.

Ballooning
Glovento Sur
Tel: 958 29 03 16; www.gloventosur.com
Balloon flights in the Granada region (Granada city, Guadix, Sierra Nevada, Antequera and elsewhere).

Golf
The Costa del Sol has been dubbed the Costa del Golf, because it has many of the region's best golf courses. The Federación Andaluza de Golf has more than 50 courses in Andalucía, including Huelva, Cádiz, Jerez, Málaga and Almería. Its website has information in Spanish and English.
Federación Andaluza de Golf
Tel: 952 22 55 90; www.fga.org

You can hire pedalos in many resorts

Horse riding
Dallas Love
Horse-riding expeditions around Bubión, Alpujarras.
Tel: 958 76 30 38; www.spain-horse-riding.com
Los Alamos
Barbate, on the coast of Cádiz.
Tel: 956 43 74 16;
www.losalamosriding.co.uk
Nerja Riding Holidays
Tours inland from the eastern Costa del Sol.
Tel: 952 52 30 18;
www.nerjaridingholidays.com

The El Gato cave system outside Benaoján

Nautical
El Cabo a Fondo
Expeditions by semi-rigid inflatables to parts of the spectacular El Cabo de Gata peninsula, otherwise inaccessible by land.
Cabo de Gata. Tel: 950 37 13 46;
www.elcaboafondo.com

Skiing
For three to four months each winter, depending on regional weather patterns, **Pradollano** in the Sierra Nevada east of Granada becomes Europe's most southerly ski resort (*see p124*). Only half an hour by bus from Granada, the (rather modest) resort has over 50 slopes from nursery to black runs, skiboard runs, toboggan and sledging routes, as well as accommodation ranging from youth hostels to four-star hotels. The resort has online reservations and an interactive phone line offering weather reports and reservations.

Skydiving
Skydivespain
Accompanied 'tandem' parachute jumps, full, 'accelerated free fall' courses for skydiver qualification, and powered parachute flights.
Tel: 666 11 81 52; www.skydivespain.com

Specialist tours
For tours and activities in Cazorla nature reserve, see pp130–31.

Monte Aventura
Specialist in four-wheel safaris and activity pursuits in the Sierra de las Nieves.
Tel: 952 88 15 19. www.monteaventura.com

RENFE's network of regional trains will get you from Algeciras to Jaén, and from Almería to Huelva, usually via Bobadilla

Walking
Andalucían Adventures
Walking holidays across Andalucía.
Tel: 01453 834 137 (UK);
www.andalucian-adventures.co.uk
Walking Wild Andalucía
Tel: 951 16 00 49;
www.walkingwildandalucia.com

Indoor pursuits
Flamenco
Dance Holidays
Tel: 01206 577 000 (UK).
Viva Flamenco
Holidays, workshops and classes.

Tel: 08700 113 347 (UK);
www.vivaflamencopromotions.com

Food and drink
The Atelier
Vegetarian and vegan hotel offering cookery courses by award-winning chef Jean-Claude Juston, author of *The New Spain: Vegan and Vegetarian Restaurants in Spain*, in this hamlet.
Mecina Fondales, Alpujarras.
Tel: 958 85 75 01; www.ivu.org/atelier
Exclusive Wine Vacations
Tel: (877) 485 7221 (USA);
www.exclusivewinevacations.com

Shopping

Spain has joined the rest of the Eurozone states in a gradual levelling of prices in the wake of 1 January 2002 and the arrival of the euro. Like them it has also experienced a rounding up of prices – although this is not surprising when currency units changed so drastically.

Seville street stall

Shoes, clothes, CDs, most foods, alcohol and cigarettes remain cheaper in Spain than in northern Europe. Books, stereos, computers and kitchen equipment are more expensive. IVA (*Impuesto Sobre el Valor Añadido* – value added tax) is applied at two rates, 16% or 7% depending on the goods or services in question, and can also make a difference

to prices, which are often marked up *sin IVA* (without VAT). Most tourist shops usually offer tax-free shopping for non-EU citizens.

Seville, Granada and Marbella, and to a lesser extent Cádiz, Córdoba, Jaén, Jerez and Málaga, have shopping districts to match any northern European city.

El Corte Inglés
Spain's homegrown department store is a good one-stop shop for almost everything you need including clothes, electrical goods, toiletries, books, magazines and newspapers in English, and maps. There is usually a supermarket, too, which stocks gourmet and imported international foods. The emphasis is on quality rather than rock-bottom prices; it may not be the cheapest place in town but there again it is rarely the most expensive. There are branches of El Corte Inglés in Seville (five), Cádiz, Algeciras, Córdoba, Granada, Huelva, Jaén, Jerez de la Frontera, Linares, Málaga and Marbella.

Books
Lavish production values make Spanish books objects of desire, although foreign-language editions are rare.

Azulejos – beautifully painted and glazed tiles

University cities such as Seville have at least one store with a foreign-language section, notably the excellent **Vertice** opposite the university (*calle San Fernando 33; tel: 954 21 16 54*). English books are widely available on the Costa del Sol where there are even foreign-language bookshops such as Nerja Book Centre (*calle Granada 30–32, Nerja; tel: 952 52 09 08*).

Andalucía's food and drink are among the most distinctive in Spain

Clothing

It takes immense cool to carry off wearing Spanish men's hats and even more so the *mantilla* and *peinata* (shawl and ornamental comb), but if you can they're worth the expense. *Gitano* dresses and *trajes de luces* are other popular souvenirs.

Crafts

The cities and countryside are excellent hunting grounds for crafts, both indigenous and imported. Andalucía produces numerous forms of glazed and matt pottery, as well as its forest regions' superb (if costly) olive and oak wood products.

Food

There remain foodstuffs, such as olive oils and cured meats, that are uniquely Spanish and even uniquely Andalucían. Jaén is said to be the largest olive-growing region on the planet, and country lanes are full of signs offering virgin oil for sale. Similarly, the Atlantic Costa de la Luz is famed for its tuna, sardines and other fish, which can be found on delicatessen counters.

The range of fresh and preserved foodstuffs is vast and varies enormously across Andalucía. Spain's commendable resistance to processing and factory production ensures that its food is among the finest in Europe.

Music and videos

New and best-selling CDs, DVDs and videos sell at similar prices to northern Europe, but back catalogues can often be a fraction of the recommended retail price, as can recordable software such as CD-Rs and DVD-Rs.

Entertainment

Andalucía offers a generous choice of entertainment from low- to high-brow, depending on your taste. Given the climate, the best things happen outside and it's common to see music, dance and theatre on open-air stages in public places. There are even open-air 'summer' cinemas where you can watch the latest Hollywood film in the cool of the night under the stars.

Agencies specialising in booking tickets for all entertainments include *www.entradas.com; tel: 902 22 16 22* and *www.servicaixa.com; tel: 902 33 22 11.*

Flamenco *bailadora*, dancer

The Andalucían thirst for culture can be seen in the proliferating number of arts festivals, galleries and venues, and the pages of journalism dedicated to these at national, regional and local levels.

FLAMENCO

Many visitors to Andalucía hope to get a taste of authentic flamenco music and dance (*see pp18–19*). The discussion about what is and isn't authentic flamenco could go on forever. A die-hard flamenco expert would say that if a foreign tourist is watching it, it isn't the real thing; that the *duende* only appears spontaneously, behind closed doors, among gypsies and their friends. But it could easily be argued that flamenco is in constant evolution, has hybridised in a thousand equally valid ways and that it is, when it is reduced to its essentials, a form of entertainment. In short, be discerning when choosing a show to see, avoiding those which are obviously geared up to receive tour parties, and

you'll see something close to the real thing. There are venues in all major Andalucían cities and lists of them are available from local tourist information offices. Prices are generally not cheap, but often a drink or dinner is included.

Seville

Triana claims to be the home of flamenco and there are several bars there giving impromptu or unadvertised shows. The better-known flamenco venues, however, are all in Santa Cruz. They include the new Museo del Baile Flamenco (*see p35*) and the following:

Casa de la Memoria de Al Andalus

A cultural centre dedicated to Andalucían traditional culture in general but especially flamenco, with shows nightly at 9pm.

Calle Ximenez de Enciso 28. Tel: 954 56 06 70.

La Carbonería

A bar in what were once a coal merchant's premises which has long had

Costa del Sol
Complejo Cinematográfico Gran
Marbella
Between Hipercor and Puerto Banús.
Tel: 952 81 64 21.

Granada
Centro de Lenguas Modernas
(University of Granada)
Placeta del Hospicio Viejo.
Tel: 958 21 56 60.
Cine Club Universitario
Facultad de Ciencias. Tel: 958 24 34 84.

Inside the Gran Teatro de Córdoba

Children

Anyone travelling with children in Andalucía will meet a particularly warm welcome almost everywhere. Children are integrated into Spanish social life to the extent that they can often be seen out with their parents until the small hours.

Children will enjoy the fiestas

There's no shortage of activities for kids on the Costa del Sol, and most parts of the coast and the major cities are within reach of a waterpark. Combining cultural sightseeing with keeping children occupied, however, may pose a challenge. The mosque at Córdoba and the Alhambra offer the challenge of finding your way around, and castles and caves can also be fun to explore. Many fiestas include spectacles especially for children, but all of them can be entertaining.

Gibraltar
For its cable car and monkeys.
See pp72–3.

Isla Mágica
Andalucía's premier theme park with white knuckle and gentler rides, themed areas and shows.
See p48.

Mini-Hollywood
The oldest of various Wild West theme attractions in the Tabernas area of Almería, and the place where they shot parts of *The Magnificent Seven, A Fistful of Dollars, The Good, the Bad and the Ugly* and dozens of other spaghetti westerns. There are Wild West extravaganzas, cancan shows and a small zoo with events throughout the day.
See pp108–9.

La Rábida
The key Columbus site is now a museum with historical displays and, at the *muelle* (jetty), there are life-sized models of his ships to explore.
See pp64–5.

Parque de las Ciencias, Granada
Hands-on science park on the city outskirts, with planetarium, science games and various exhibitions pitched at bloodthirsty pre-teens. The planetarium also has viewings at its observatory depending on sky conditions and season.
Avenida del Mediterráneo.
Tel: 958 13 19 00.
www.parqueciencias.com. Open: Tue–Sat 10am–7pm, Sun 10am–3pm.
Admission charge (separate charge for planetarium).

Real Escuela Andaluz de Arte Ecuestre
See p53.

Isla Magica theme park

SELWO Aventura

Andalucía's largest wildlife park, with tours and aerial walkways through outdoor areas where animals dwell in habitats resembling 'natural' conditions. *Off A7 motorway Las Lomas Del Monte/Estepona. Tel: 902 19 04 82. Open: 10am–6pm (until 8pm in summer). Admission charge. Group and other reductions including Selwopack joint admission to Marina and Telecabinas (see below).*

SELWO Marina

Aquarium attraction with dolphins, sea lions and penguins. *Parque de la Paloma, Benalmádena. Tel: 902 19 04 82. Open: 10am–6pm (later in summer). Admission charge.*

Telecabinas Benalmádena

Panoramic cable-car rides into the hills above Torremolinos, where there are viewpoints and marked walks.

Esplanada Tivoli, Benalmádena. Tel: 902 19 04 82; www.teleferico.com. Open: daily 10.30am–6pm. Closed: mid-Jan–mid-Feb. Admission charge. Does not run in bad weather – call for confirmation.

Tivoli World

The largest theme park on the Costa del Sol, with white knuckle and gentler rides, gardens and shows. *Avenida de Tivoli, Arroyo de la Miel, Benalmádena. Tel: 952 57 70 16; www.tivoli-es. Open: daily 6pm–2am (weekends only Oct–Nov). Closed: Dec–Mar. Admission charge (children under 1m (3ft 3ins) free admission).*

Wheel of Seville

A 60m (197ft) tall wheel with 42 enclosed cabins giving sweeping views of the city. *www.noriapanoramicadesevilla.com. Open: 10am–midnight. Admission charge.*

Taking care of Jerez's grapes

Food and drink

Andalucía's landscape and climate have won an unrivalled reputation for the region's food and drink. Several Spanish classics originate here, and its restaurant owners have recently been making inroads into that preserve of French and more northerly establishments, the Michelin and other guides.

What to eat

It is the home of *gazpacho*, the tomato-based chilled vegetable soup, and *rabo de toro*, the oxtail stew that might be considered the consummate Andalucían *plato*. The region's fishing fleets have access to two oceans, and its vegetable growers have turned its eastern half into a giant hothouse for subtropical fruit

Jamón, ham, hangs air drying for at least a year

and vegetables, and the western half into lush cereal-growing areas and farmland. With the exceptions of Jerez de la Frontera and Montilla, Andalucía was a late starter in the wine sector, but it has produced several whites and now a number of reds that are winning plaudits from critics. Málaga's modest Larios distillery produces a world-class gin that many aficionados prefer over well-known British brands.

Vegetarian and vegan foods
The situation for vegetarian and vegan eaters in Spain is improving. Most fair-sized towns have a vegetarian restaurant and many of the better restaurants will, forewarned, cater even for vegans – but sometimes vegetarian travellers have to make do with staples such as soups and omelettes. It's best to double-check vegetarian-sounding dishes, as they can sometimes be flavoured with ham or cod, or with animal stock.

Typical meals and ingredients
Specialities can vary from region to region, even village to village, but Andalucían farmers' perseverance with traditional methods produces fresh

meats and vegetables wherever you eat or shop. Fish from the Atlantic and Mediterranean reaches shops and restaurants within a matter of hours. Below are some typical foods you'll encounter across Andalucía.

Aceitunas olives, the ubiquitous pre-meal nibble: *verde* (green) or *negro* (black), and sometimes *relleno* (stuffed), with *pimiento* (pepper) or *pepinillos* (baby gherkins).

Aguacate avocado, often served with *vinaigre* (vinaigrette), *con gambas* (with prawns) and occasionally but deliciously as a *sopa* (soup).

Ajo blanco white garlic soup served chilled, often strong; perfect hot on a cold day (and proof of food writer Katherine Whitehorn's dictum, 'If your friends don't like garlic, change your friends').

Albondigas meatballs, often spicy, in a rich onion and herb or tomato sauce.

Alcachofas artichokes, sometimes with *vinaigre* (vinaigrette), *a la andaluz* (with bacon and ham) or *romana* (battered and fried).

Almejas clams, often *a la marinero* (in white wine and herbs).

Almendras almonds, found almost everywhere in Andalucía as tapas and in desserts such as *tarta* (flan), or sometimes as part of a *salsa* (sauce) for *pollo* (chicken).

Alubias beans cooked in *estofados* (stews) and *sopas*.

Anchoas anchovies, a common *tapa* in vinegar, but often found in *montaditos* (small bread rolls), containing *queso* and pimiento. Also known as **boquerones**.

Apio celery, used in *estofados* and *sopas* or *asado* (baked).

Atún tuna, famously from the Costa de la Luz, often *al horno* (baked in the oven), or in *ensalata mixta* (mixed salad), which may be served automatically as a pre-meal taster.

Bacalao cod: *a la plancha* (grilled), *frito* (fried), or in stews and soups.

Berenjenas aubergine or eggplant, usually sliced or chipped, fried, sometimes battered.

Besugo bream, given a similar treatment to *bacalao* (cod).

Calabacin and **calabaza** courgette/marrow, and pumpkin, served as vegetables or a classic country soup.

Calamares squid, often *frito*, *romano*, or *en su tinta* (cooked in its own ink).

Cangrejo crab.

Two oceans provide Andalucía with its definitive seafood dish, paella, originally from Valencia

Seville's excellent Egaña Oriza

Cerdo pork.

Champiñones and **setas** mushrooms, a frequent *tapa*. *Champiñones* are commonly the larger button variety, *setas* wild woodland fungi.

Chorizo spicy red sausages, cold and sliced as a *tapa*, cooked with *patatas fritas* (fries/chips) and often diced into *estofados*.

Chuletas chops, of *cordero* (lamb) or *cerdo* (pork).

Codorniz quail, a speciality of country restaurants – *huevos de codornices* (quail's eggs) are a delicious *tapa*, individually fried and served on bread with *jamón* (ham).

Conejo rabbit, commonly served as an *estofado*, with *garbanzos* (chickpeas).

Croquetas breaded potato croquettes *relleno* (stuffed) with chicken, ham or *espinaca* (spinach).

Esparragos asparagus, which grows wild all over Andalucía and is served steamed or fried.

Guisantes green garden peas.

Habas broad beans.

Huevos eggs: *duro* (hardboiled), *frito* (fried), *revuelta* (scrambled, usually with something else) or *rancheros*, in a spicy tomato sauce with *chorizo* and *alubias*.

Lechuga lettuce, mainstay of any *ensalada*.

Lenguado sole, most popular fish after *bacalao*, cooked in various ways.

Lentejas lentils, of various colours, used in soups or vegetable stews.

Mariscos seafood, but more correctly shellfish, often as a *variados* (a variety of shellfish cooked in wines and herbs), or *sopa*.

Merluza hake, cooked *a la plancha* or in a variety of sauces.

Morcilla a robust country sausage whose closest English equivalent is black pudding. It's eaten sliced thin as a cold *tapa*, or hot with a *salsa*, *patatas* and *verduras* (green vegetables).

Pato duck.

Pavo turkey.

Pechuga de pollo the most common way chicken arrives at your table: roast breast, a generous helping usually cooked in its own juices.

Perdiz like quail, pheasant is a popular country dish, often served with *alubias*.

Pez espado literally 'sword fish', customarily served as unadorned steaks, but these days an endangered species.

Pulpo, pulpito octopus and baby octopus, smaller and more tender than the sea monsters served in regions such as Galicia.

Queso cheese: not an Andalucían strong point, with *manchego* (from La Mancha) the most common, but country-made *queso de cabra* (goat's cheese) is a great starter and a *tapa* to be sought out.

Rape monkfish, also popular, and served with wine or herb sauces.

Raya skate, served *a la plancha* or with sauces.

Sardinas sardines. A typical way to cook these (and many other types of fish and seafood) in beach restaurants is to barbecue them on skewers, *al espeto*.

Solomillo better-quality beef steak, served *al vino* (in red wine sauce) or simply *con patatas fritas* (steak and chips).

Sopa soup, a country staple and a sophisticated starter in many city restaurants. Most common are *sopa de pescado* (mixed fish) and *sopa de verduras*. *Sopa de calabaza* (pumpkin) can be very tasty.

Ternera veal, commonly in *patas* (leg of), or *estofado* (stew) or with *alubias* (beans).

Tortilla omelette. A Spanish staple in bars everywhere, and a good stop-gap for vegetarians, is *tortilla de patata*, potato omelette.

Sardines *al espeto*

Alfresco dining in Marbella

Where to eat

Andalucíans eat late by the rest of Europe's standards. Lunch, the main meal of the day, is from 2pm onwards. After an afternoon *merienda* around 5–7pm, which can be something savoury but usually sweet, dinner falls between 9 and 11pm. Many people prefer a light snack or a round of tapas with friends in one or more bars, rather than a sit-down dinner.

Restaurants in Andalucía vary from the humble beach bar or *chiringuito* serving barbecued fish almost straight out of the sea, to starched temples of haute cuisine in Seville, Granada and Córdoba. Prices generally vary according to the pretensions of the owners, but they are not always a good guide to quality.

When choosing a restaurant the best advice is to eat where the locals eat and avoid anywhere that displays photographs of its dishes outside. Some rural *ventas* and roadside truck stops serve excellent *menús del día* at a price you couldn't argue with – a full car park is usually a guarantee that you will eat well within. No restaurant imposes a dress code on its clientele, but if you don't want to feel out of place, dress informal-smart for any mid-price to expensive restaurant.

In the following list of recommended restaurants, the price symbols indicate the approximate cost per head of a typical meal without drinks:

★   up to €15
★★   up to €30
★★★   over €30

Almería

Café Alcazar ★★

One of the most popular bar-restaurants in the Puerta Purchena district at the heart of the old town, with a wide range of seafood tapas and *platos*.
Calle Almería 2.
Tel: 950 23 89 95.

Los Mariscos ★

Sturdy beer-and-tapas fish bar-restaurant, the place to eat with the locals.
Calle Mendez Nuñez 20.
Tel: 950 23 54 02.

Mesa España ★★

One of the best mid-range restaurants in Almería, offering fish, meat and vegetarian alternatives.
Calle Mendez Nuñez 19.
Tel: 950 27 49 28.

Taberna Torreluz ★★

A great central place for tapas and drinks, and the most informal of the three restaurants linked to the hotel of the same name. No need to book.
Plaza Flores 3. Tel: 950 23 43 99.

Valentin ★★★

Probably the most upmarket restaurant in town, with an extensive menu of delicately prepared fish and seafood dishes, and a complement of meat and international dishes.

Andalucía's restaurants often have the pick of local produce

Tenor Iribarne 19.
Tel: 950 26 44 75.

Antequera

Los Dolmenes ★

Convenient before or after visiting the dolmens on the edge of town, with a cool dining room in which local food is served.
Cruz El Romeral.
Tel: 952 84 59 56.

Arcos de la Frontera

El Convento ★★

The best restaurant in town, in an extraordinary 16th-century palace setting. Perfect for trying some regional specialities, not least *perdiz en almendras* (pheasant in almond sauce).
Calle Marqués de Torresoto 7.
Tel: 956 70 32 22.

Benaoján

El Molino del Santo ★★

One of the most idyllic restaurant settings in Andalucía: under willow trees by a mill stream in the gardens of a mountain-hideout hotel. Offers a wide range of local specialities using organic ingredients, with plenty to please every taste.
Benaoján.
Tel: 952 16 71 51.

Cádiz

1800 ★★

A Cádiz institution, and somewhat cheaper and easier to book into than El Faro, with a near definitive *bacalao pil-pil* (cod in garlic).
Paseo Maritimo 3.
Tel: 956 26 02 03.

El Faro ★–★★★

Possibly the most fabulous fish restaurant in Andalucía, and certainly the most fabled. Book for the pricier upstairs restaurant, just roll up for the friendly downstairs tapas bar, and some wonderful variations on fish and seafood in either.

Nothing can beat a beach barbecue

Calle San Felix 15.
Tel: 902 21 10 68.

El Sardinero ★

Handsomely positioned in this small square, this is a favourite snack and takeaway restaurant for great fish, and the nearest *gaditanos* get to English takeaway fish and chips.
Plaza San Juan de Dios 5.
Tel: 956 26 33 37.

Ventorrillo del Chato ★★

Dating in parts from the 1780s, this is said to have been the place where tapas was invented, and in the 1820s was King Fernando VII's favourite restaurant.
Via Augusta Julia
Tel: 956 25 00 25.

Cómpeta

El Pilón ★

British-owned restaurant serving a filling and good-value *menú del día* on its terrace, with views over the rooftops and the surrounding hills. Good choices for vegetarians.
Calle Laberinto.
Tel: 952 55 35 12.

Córdoba

Almudaina ★★

One of the finest of Córdoba's restaurants, and the place to try some of the most typical Córdoban dishes, *rabo de toro* (oxtail) and *salmorejo*, a thick gazpacho-like vegetable soup or stew.
Plaza Campo Santo de los Martires 1.
Tel: 957 47 43 42.

El Caballo Rojo ★★

The most famous restaurant in the city, specialising in local dishes dating from Moorish times, many of which still influence modern Andalucían cooking. The cheaper/quicker tapas bar is also recommended.
Calle Cardenal Herrero 28.
Tel: 957 47 53 75.

El Churrasco ★★★

This smart restaurant completes Córdoba's trio of top-notch restaurants, and is famed for its titular

pork dish, *churrasco*, in a pepper sauce.
Calle Romero 16.
Tel: 957 29 08 19.

Gaucín
La Fructuosa ★
The cosy dining room, arranged around an old wine press, extends on to the patio from which there are views of Gibraltar and the African coast.
Calle Convento 67.
Tel: 952 15 10 72.

Gibraltar
Claus on the Rock ★★
Smart seafront restaurant with an international menu and the place where most Rock inhabitants head for a celebration.
Queensway Quay.
Tel: 48686.
Lord Nelson ★
The best of the restaurants in the town's central meeting place.
10 Casemates Square.
Tel: 50009.

Granada
Arrayanes ★★
One of the best north African restaurants in the Albaicín, sumptuously decorated and specialising in *tagines*, sturdy meat, fish or vegetable stews.
Cuesta Marañas 4.
Tel: 958 22 84 01.

The dining room of Córdoba's venerable eaterie El Caballo Rojo

Cuñini ★★
Excellent seafood from Andalucía and also Galicia, this smart restaurant off Bib-Rambla also has a cheap and friendly tapas bar.
Plaza Pescaderia 14.
Tel: 958 25 07 77.
Las Tinajas ★★
One of Granada's smartest restaurants, with a mix of southern and northern Spanish classics, and some fine fish dishes. Also handy for Bib-Rambla.
Calle Martinez Campos 17. Tel: 958 25 43 93.
Parador de San Francisco ★★
A place to splash out and enjoy almost unrivalled views of the Albaicín from the garden terrace.
Real de la Alhambra.
Tel: 958 22 14 40.

Pilar de Toro ★★
Classic *grenadino* dishes in this elegant, converted 17th-century mansion, which has a downstairs tapas bar and upstairs restaurant with its own terrace.
Hospital de Santa Ana 12 (just off Plaza Nueva).
Tel: 958 22 38 47.

Grazalema
Cadiz el Chico ★★
The best restaurant in the rainiest village in Spain, remodelled with pine, still serving excellent food, including a splendid *pierna de cordero* (leg of lamb) for two, a scorching *sopa de ajo*, and, in season, dishes with *tagarniñas* (wild thistles).
Plaza de España.
Tel: 956 13 22 40.

Andalucía has a reputation as Spain's vegetable garden

Málaga

Antonio Martin ★★★
One of Málaga's oldest
fish restaurants, and one
of the most expensive.
Plaza la Malagueta 16.
Tel: 952 22 73 98.

**El Vegetariano de la
Alcazabilla ★★**
Fairly smart vegetarian
restaurant next to Albéniz
cinema (handy for the
Picasso Museum and the
Alcazaba), with vegan
dishes available.
Pozo del Rey 5.
Tel: 952 21 48 58.

Marbella

Il Cantuccio ★★
Hidden in an alleyway off
calle Ancha this great
little Italian restaurant is

one of Marbella's best-
kept secrets.
Callejón Santo Cristo 3.
Tel: 952 77 04 92.

La Comedia ★★
Pan-global dishes – from
the Arctic circle to
Macronesia – served with
style and wit in this
trendy but friendly
designer restaurant
hidden in a corner of
one of the *casco antiguo*'s
old squares.
Booking advised.
Plaza de la Victoria 3.
Tel: 952 77 64 78.

Ronda

Pedro Romero ★★
Ronda's shrine to
bullfighting with real
bulls' heads on the walls

and photographs of
Hemingway and Welles
hanging out with
bullfighting heroes such
as Antonio Ordoñez.
The menu is somewhat
upmarket, but it's still the
place to try classics such
as *rabo de toro*, *perdiz* and
conejo.
Virgen de la Paz 18.
Tel: 952 87 11 10.

Puerta Grande ★
This relatively new arrival
in a restaurant-heavy
town has subtle variations
on salmon in leek sauce,
and *berenjenas con miel*
(fried aubergine with
honey).
Calle Nueva 10.
Tel: 952 87 92 00.

Tragabuches ★★★
Unbeaten the length
and breadth of Andalucía,
this Michelin-starred
temple of *nueva cocida*
goes from strength to
strength and has a
Michelin star for its
unique mix of local
ingredients and
traditional dishes mixed
in outrageous new ways.
José Aparicio 1.
Tel: 952 19 02 91.

Sanlúcar de Barrameda

Casa Bigote ★★
The place to taste
Sanluqueña food: a
seafront bar and

restaurant in the traditional Bajo de Guia fishermen's *barrio* from which there is a view across the water to Doñana National Park.
Bajo de Guia.
Tel: 956 36 26 96.

Mirador Doñana ★★
This upmarket neighbour to the Bigote has a less funky take on Sanlúcar's traditional fish and seafood.
Bajo de Guia.
Tel: 956 36 42 05.

Seville

Corral del Agua ★★
Stylish courtyard restaurant in an alley by the Alcázar walls, with a menu veering towards *nueva cocida*.
Callejón del Agua 6.
Tel: 954 22 48 41.

Egaña Oriza ★★–★★★
One of the smartest restaurants in town, with a *nueva cocida* menu (boar with pears and prunes), on a corner of the Alcázar gardens and Plaza Don Juan de Austria. The wonderful tapas bar is highly recommended.
Calle San Fernando 41.
Tel: 954 22 72 54.

El Kiosco de las Flores ★
A Triana institution, on the riverside, this is one

of *the* places to taste fish in Seville.
Calle del Betis.
Tel: 954 27 45 76.

Enrique Becerra ★★
Unassuming backstreet tapas bar and restaurant popular with locals and the *New York Times* food pages.
Calle Gamazo 2.
Tel: 954 21 30 49.

Hosteria El Laurel ★★
Busy and popular traditional restaurant below the eponymous hotel in a square in Santa Cruz. Baked meats and fish are a speciality, with an excellent *friturada variada* (batter-fried seafood selection).
Plaza de los Venerables 5.
Tel: 954 22 02 95.

La Albahaca ★★★
This converted mansion with movie-set interiors has an excellent if expensive traditional menu.
Plaza Santa Cruz 12.
Tel: 954 22 07 14.

Taberna del Alabardero ★★
Another impressive mansion conversion, with a light international menu.
Calle Zaragoza 20.
Tel: 954 50 27 21.

Tarifa

Arte Vida ★
Hotel-restaurant-gallery just north of Tarifa, with a beach restaurant specialising in grilled fish, meats, salad and pizzas.
Carretera N340.
Tel: 956 68 52 46.

Casa Amarilla ★
Classic Andalucían bodega specialising in local ham, tuna and cheese in the centre of Tarifa's Sancho IV party zone.
Sancho IV El Bravo 9.
Tel: 956 68 19 93.

The Terrace ★★
Probably the best restaurant on the Tarifa beach, set in the dense subtropical gardens of the trendy Hurricane Hotel.
Hotel Hurricane,
carretera N340.
Tel: 956 68 49 19.

Úbeda ★★
El Marqués
This restaurant is in one of Úbeda's two smartest hotels, a 16th-century mansion conversion. The menu specialises in traditional *Úbense* recipes using local meat, vegetables and fish from the coast.
Hotel Maria de Molino,
Plaza del Ayuntamiento.
Tel: 953 79 53 56.

Hotels and accommodation

Andalucía is the most popular tourist destination in Spain and both the number and quality of hotels are increasing to meet that demand. Some more industrial cities such as Huelva and Málaga are still poorly served with visitor accommodation, while some of the smallest *pueblos* now boast international quality boutique hotels.

Parador in Carmona

Below is a selection of mid-range to higher hotels across Andalucía which can be assumed to have en suite facilities and take most credit cards. For information on hostels and camping, *see p185*.

Booking
Booking is advisable whenever possible, and an absolute must if you plan to visit during *Semana Santa*, or any other local festivity.

Hotels will hold rooms until 8pm or later if you warn them of your estimated arrival time, but some may require pre-booking by credit card. Be warned that many do not quote prices inclusive of 17 per cent IVA, Spain's value added tax. Checkout is usually at noon, but most hotels will keep bags or even let you use the room until later if asked.

Prices
The prices shown according to the star system opposite are average summertime prices (although many hotels have year-round prices) for a double room. Suites and rooms during premium periods will be extra.

★	under €50
★★	€50–100
★★★	€100–150
★★★★	€150–250

Almería
AM Torreluz ★★★
This is one of the smartest hotels in the city. All mod cons, gym, sauna, spa and small rooftop terrace with pool.
Plaza Flores 5. Tel: 902 23 49 99; www.amhoteles.com

Gran Hotel Almería ★★★
Large four-star convention-type hotel dating from the 1960s. Restaurant, bars, pool, but in a noisy part of town.
Avenida Reina Regente 8.
Tel: 950 23 80 11;
www.granhotelalmeria.com

La Perla ★★
Almería's oldest hotel, now refurbished, and a friendly budget option.
Plaza del Carmen 7. Tel: 950 23 88 77;
www.githotels.com

Vincci Mediterráneo ★★★
The trendiest hotel in Almería, with rooms and public spaces verging on *minimalista* style. Business facilities available.

Avenida del Mediterráneo 369.
Tel: 950 62 42 72; www.vincci-hotels.com

Arcos de la Frontera
El Convento ★★
The best option in a town with few
decent hotels. As the name suggests, this
is a converted 17th-century convent on
the edge of the precipice on which Arcos
sits.
Calle Maldonado 2. Tel: 956 70 23 33;
www.webdearcos/elconvento
Marqués de Torresoto ★★
More historic splendour in this
renovated mansion with a patio
overlooking the view.
Calle Marqués de Torresoto 4.
Tel: 956 70 07 17; www.hmdetorresoto.com

Benaoján
El Molino del Santo ★★
Very pleasant English-owned country
house hotel near Ronda, with small
bungalow-type rooms in mature
gardens, an outdoor pool and lovely
restaurant under willows by a tumbling
mountain stream.
Estación de Benaoján/Montejaque.
Tel: 952 16 71 51;
www.molinodelsanto.com.
Closed: mid-Nov–mid-Feb.

Benarrabá
Banú Rabbah ★★
Launched as a collective by young
people from this tiny *Pueblo Blanco*,
this is the only hotel between Ronda
and Gaucín. Twelve rooms, some with
views over the mountains and all with
spacious terraces.
Calle Sierra Bermeja.
Tel: 952 15 02 88; www.hbenarraba.es

Bubión
Las Terrazas ★
Spartan but comfortable and friendly
family-run hotel with views to the south
of this Alpujarran village.
Plaza del Sol 7. Tel: 958 76 30 34;
www.terrazasalpujarra.com

Cádiz
Francia y Paris ★★
The best mid-range option in the old
town, a central, quiet, if anonymous
modern hotel behind a beautiful *belle
époque* façade.
Plaza de San Francisco 6.
Tel: 956 21 23 19; www.hotelfrancia.com
Playa Victoria ★★★
Best of the beachside hotels in
'downtown' new Cádiz with stylish
rooms and suites, all with sea views.
Glorieta Ingeniero la Cierva 4.
Tel: 956 20 51 00;
www.palafoxhoteles.com

Carmona
Alcázar de la Reina ★★★
One of Carmona's fabulous 16th-
century mansions, sumptuously
renovated and sensitively modernised.
Plaza de Lasso 2. Tel: 954 19 62 00;
www.alcazar-reina.es
La Casa de Carmona ★★★★
Gorgeous 16th-century palace
conversion in the beautiful town centre,
decorated with antiques and paintings.
Plaza de Lasso 1. Tel: 954 19 10 00;
www.casadecarmona.com

Cazorla
Villa Turistica de Cazorla ★★
Very pleasant hotel just on the edge of
this mountain town, a short walk from

A room at the Acinipo hotel, Ronda

the centre, with restaurant, gardens, pools and views of the town.
Ladera de San Isicio. Tel: 953 71 01 00; www.villacazorla.com

Conil de la Frontera
Fuerte Conil ★★★
Part of the Fuerte chain which has hotels in Marbella and Grazalema, this is the most comfortable of the Costa de la Luz beach hotels, a large complex above the beach with pools and restaurants. Very popular with German and British visitors.
Playa de la Fontanilla. Tel: 956 44 33 44; www.fuertehotels.com

Córdoba
Amistad Córdoba ★★★
Tastefully modernised conversion of two 18th-century mansions on the edge of La Juderia, the former Jewish *barrio*, with a Mudéjar-style patio.
Plaza de Maimonides 3. Tel: 957 42 03 35; www.nh-hotels.com

El Triunfo ★★
Probably the best mid-price option here, a friendly, traditional hotel on the eastern side of the Mezquita, with bar and restaurant and some rooms with Mezquita views.
Calle Corregidor Luis de la Cerda 79. Tel: 957 49 84 84; www.htriunfo.com
González ★★
Former Moorish palace by the Mezquita, with rooms looking onto a whitewashed interior patio.
Calle Manrique 3. Tel: 957 47 98 19.

Frigiliana
Los Caracoles ★★
Highly original hotel composed of five snail-inspired bungalows, each sleeping up to four people. In the pretty region of the Axarquia.
Carretera Frigiliana–Torrox, km 4.6. Tel: 952 03 06 09; www.hotelloscaracoles.com

Gaucín
Casablanca ★★★
Handsome mansion conversion with gardens, pool and mock-Arabic mirador.
Calle Llana 12. Tel: 952 15 10 19; www.casablanca-gaucin.com
La Fructuosa ★★
Five elegant modern suites with large terraces looking down towards the Rock and Africa.
Calle Convento 67. Tel: 952 15 10 72; www.lafructuosa.com

Gibraltar
Caleta ★★★
Luxury hotel on the beach in this former fishing village at the other end of the Rock.

Catalan Bay. Tel: 76501;
www.caletahotel.com

Eliott ★★★
The smartest central hotel, popular with
business travellers.
Governor's Parade. Tel: 70500;
www.gib.gi/eliotthotel

The Rock ★★★
The Gibraltarian institution, built by the
Marquess of Bute in 1929 and totally
refurbished in 2000. All rooms sea-
facing, restaurants, bars and a pool.
Europa Road. Tel: 73000;
www.rockhotelgibraltar.com

Granada

America ★★
This is the ideal place to stay in
Granada, a lovely old mansion deep
inside the Alhambra. Booking ahead
advised.
Real de al Alhambra 53.
Tel: 958 22 74 71; www.hamerica.com

Carmen de Santa Inés ★★
Like its sister hotel the Palacio de Santa
Inés, this is an exquisitely refurbished
mansion, with suites off a column-lined
courtyard with fountain.
Placeta Porras 7. Tel: 958 22 63 80;
www.carmensantaines.com

Juan Miguel ★★
Central hotel, near the Puerta Real, and
a decent mid-range option.
Acero del Darro 24. Tel: 958 52 11 11.

Macia Plaza ★★
Pleasantly modernised townhouse hotel
on this central square.
Plaza Nueva 4. Tel: 958 22 75 36.

Palacio de Santa Inés ★★★
Renovated 16th-century mansion at the
bottom of the Albaicín, with rooms
around a beautiful courtyard.

Cuesta de Santa Inés 9.
Tel: 958 22 23 62;
www.palaciosantaines.com

Reina Cristina ★★
Handy central mid-price hotel in a fairly
quiet side street. Another restored
mansion, this is famous for being the
last abode of the poet Lorca, who was
arrested here and executed after the fall
of the Republic. (Lorca's room was
where room No 310 is now.)
Tablas 4. Tel: 958 25 32 11;
www.hotelreinacristina.com

Triunfo ★★★
Smart, modern hotel at the far end of
Gran Via, quieter than some of the more
central hotels.
Plaza del Triunfo 19. Tel: 958 20 74 44.

Grazalema

Casa de las Piedras ★
Excellent if modest hotel, with a fine
restaurant and a friendly atmosphere.
Calle las Piedras 32. Tel: 956 13 20 14;
www.casadelaspiedras.net

Puerta de la Villa ★★★
This is a stylishly renovated mansion
hotel with spectacular views, restaurant,
sauna and gym.
Plaza Pequeña 8.
Tel: 956 13 23 76;
www.grazalemahotel.com

Guadix

Pedro Antonio Alarcón ★★
Guadix is close enough to Granada or
Almería to make it a day's round trip,
but if you want to share the cave-life
experience, this unique hotel offers cave
suites, gardens and pool.
Barriada san Torcuato. Tel: 958 66 49 86;
www.cuevaspedroantonio.com

Jaén

Condestable Iranzo ★★

Central, modern and comfortable hotel in the town centre.
Paseo de la Estación 32. Tel: 953 22 28 00.

Europa ★★

Another central hotel, renovated with modernist décor.
Plaza de Belén 1. Tel: 953 22 27 00; www.husa.es

Jerez

Avenida Jerez ★★

Large, modern, convention-type hotel on one of Jerez's major boulevards, a short walk from the centre.
*Avenida Alcalde Domecq 10.
Tel: 956 34 74 11; www.nh-hotels.com*

Doña Blanca ★★

Probably the best mid-range option in Jerez, a pleasant modern hotel in a backstreet just yards from Jerez's busy central market.
Calle Bodégas 11. Tel: 956 34 87 16; www.hoteldonablanca.com

Jimena de la Frontera

El Anón ★

Hotel-restaurant, built around a warren of tiny courtyards, with a rooftop pool.
Calle Consuelo 34–40. Tel: 956 64 01 13.

Málaga

Don Curro ★★

This is one of the best hotels in Málaga: simple, modern and comfortable, set back from the busy Alameda.
Calle Sancha de Lara 7. Tel: 952 22 72 00; www.hoteldoncurro.com

Las Vegas ★★

Another decent Alameda-area option, close to the beach; modern and purpose built, with its own pool.
Paseo de Sancha 22. Tel: 952 21 77 12.

Marbella

El Faro ★

The best budget option in town: a simple, friendly, purpose-built apart-hotel on a quiet street between the beach and the main street.

Tarifa's Hurricane gardens, with pool and sea beyond

Calle Virgen del Pilar 11.
Tel: 952 77 42 30.

Fuerte ★★★

On its own avenida, rooms have partial
or full sea views; there are two pools,
a gym and spa, and a beach club.
Avenida el Fuerte. Tel: 952 92 00 00;
www.fuertehotels.com

La Morada Mas Hermosa ★★

Best mid-range hotel in Marbella,
prettily renovated in the old town with
just five individually decorated suites
around a tiny courtyard.
Calle Montenebros 16.
Tel: 952 92 44 67.

Marbella Inn ★★

Slightly more comfortable than the
Faro, with restaurant and rooftop pool.
Calle Jacinto Benavente s/n.
Tel: 952 82 54 87.

Ronda

Acinipo ★★

This mixes avant-garde design with
classic Spanish décor, and is ideally
situated away from traffic and with
excellent mountain views.
Calle José Aparicio 7. Tel: 952 16 10 02;
www.hotelacinipo.com

Alavera de los Baños ★★

Ronda's most charming hotel: a row of
19th-century tanners' cottages converted
into a Hispano-Arabic-styled hotel with
a terrace restaurant and pool.
Calle San Miguel. Tel: 952 87 91 43;
www.andalucia.com/alavera

Arriadh ★★

New five-room hotel, with gardens, pool
and great views.
Estación Arriate s/n.
Tel: 952 11 43 70;
www.andalucia.com/arriadh

Mansion living in Ronda's 17th-century
San Gabriel

Fuente de la Higuera ★★

This sumptuously renovated country
house outside Ronda is run more as a
help-yourself house party.
Partido de los Frontones. Tel: 952 11 43 55;
www.hotellafuente.com

El Juncal ★★

Cool, minimalist designer hotel, a
former *cortijo* (farmhouse) transformed
with great style under the aegis of
Tragabuches. Sauna and a wild, sloped
walk-in pool.
Carretera Ronda–El Burgo.
Tel: 952 16 11 70; www.eljuncal.com

La Casona de la Ciudad ★★

Impressively grand town mansion
conversion in the old town.
Calle Marqués de Salvatierra 5.
Tel: 952 87 95 95.

La Cazalla ★★

A short drive or cab ride out of Ronda,
on a Roman road in its own secret valley,

this incomparable little hotel has just six suites, all individually designed. Great food, wild gardens and a 12th-century plunge pool.

Tajo del Abanico, 4km (2¹/₂ miles) from Ronda. Tel: 952 11 41 75; www.lacazalladeronda.com

San Gabriel ★★

This 18th-century mansion was the first hotel in Ronda's *casco antiguo*, renovated with great care by the Peréz family, who are gracious hosts.

Calle Marqués de Muctezuma 19. Tel: 952 19 03 92.

Sanlúcar de Barrameda

Posada de Palacio ★

A short walk from the town centre, this is a former manzanilla bodega, built around a central courtyard.

Calle Caballeros 11. Tel: 956 36 48 40; www.posadadepalacio.com

Tartaneros ★★

A grand mansion from Sanlúcar's wealthier days, in a central town square, decorated with antiques.

Tartaneros 8. Tel: 956 36 20 44.

Seville

Casa Numero 7 ★★★

This small, intimate hotel is actually a private home, lovingly decorated with artefacts from the family art collection.

Calle Virgenes 7. Tel: 954 22 15 81; www.casanumero7.com

Doña Maria ★★

Handsomely remodelled townhouse.

Don Remondo 19. Tel: 954 22 49 90; www.hdmaria.com

Hosteria del Laurel ★★

A bargain in the heart of Santa Cruz, above a popular restaurant.

Plaza de los Venerables 5. Tel: 954 22 02 95; www.hosteriadellaurel.com

Las Casas de la Juderia ★★★

Exquisitely refurbished mansion, in parts dating back to the 16th century.

Plaza de Santa Maria la Blanca, callejón de Dos Hermanas 7. Tel: 954 41 51 50; www.intergrouphotels.com

Las Casas de los Mercaderes ★★★

One of the best situated hotels in this noisy city, on a pedestrian street a short walk from the cathedral.

Calle Alvarez Quintero 9–13. Tel: 954 22 58 58; www.intergrouphotels.com

Los Seises ★★★★

A stunning renovation of a 16th-century palace in the shadow of the Giralda.

Calle Segovias 6. Tel: 954 22 94 95.

San Gil ★★★

Away from the centre, this is a pleasant renovation of a 1901 townhouse with a courtyard, gardens and pool.

Calle Parras 28. Tel: 954 90 68 11; www.sevillahotelsangil.com

Simon ★★

Friendly and popular mid-price option. Another 18th-century mansion conversion, this is often busy all year round.

Garcia Vinuesa 19. Tel: 954 22 66 60; www.hotelsimonsevilla.com

Tarifa

Arte Vida ★★

Funky beach hotel, gallery and restaurant, just north of town.

Carretera N340. Tel: 956 68 52 46; www.arte-vida.com

Casa Amarilla ★★

Stylish early 19th-century apartment hotel, individually-designed suites.

Sancho IV El Bravo 9. Tel: 956 68 19 93;
www.lacasaamarilla.net

Hurricane ★★★
Notoriously difficult to book into, but
with comfortable if simple rooms,
beautiful gardens and pool.
Carretera N340 78km.
Tel: 956 68 49 19; www.hotelhurricane.com

Úbeda

María de Molina ★★
Beautifully renovated 16th-century
mansion with enclosed patio and
incredible views.
Plaza del Ayuntamiento. Tel: 953 79 53 56;
www.hotelmaria-de-molina.com

Palacio de Rambla ★★
Authentic 16th-century *palacio* on the
edge of Úbeda's old town.
Plaza del Marqués 1. Tel: 953 75 01 96;
www.palaciodelarambla.com

Vejer de la Frontera
Convento San Francisco ★
Converted convent at the heart of this
gorgeous *Pueblo Blanco.*
La Plazuela. Tel: 956 45 10 01;
www.tugasa.com

La Casa del Califa ★★
The folks from Tarifa's Hurricane have
restyled this beautiful old property into
an elegant boutique hotel.
Plaza de España 16.
Tel: 956 44 77 30;
www.lacasadelcalifa.com

Zahara de la Sierra
Marqués de Zahara ★
Friendly family-run mansion
conversion is the best-kept secret
among the *Pueblos Blancos.*
Calle San Juan 3.
Tel: 956 12 30 61.

De-stress in style at Fuente de la Higuera

Practical guide

Arriving and getting around
Entry formalities
Visitors from EU countries, Iceland and Norway can enter Spain with a valid national identity card, although visitors from countries without ID cards such as Britain need a valid passport. Citizens of Australia, Canada, New Zealand and the USA do not need visas if they are staying for no more than 90 days. It is always advisable to confirm current visa regulations, either with a tour company, airline or consulate, before travelling.

In theory, anyone planning to stay in Spain for more than 90 days should report to the police to register their presence. In reality, nobody does. The situation changes if you intend to live and work in Spain, which will involve registering your residency and negotiating the Spanish employment,

You will find tourist information at every airport and major rail station

tax and welfare systems. However, the government is currently planning to simplify matters for EU citizens travelling and working in Spain. People visiting purely for leisure purposes should have no fear of Spanish bureaucracy.

By air
Andalucía has five major international airports – Almería, Granada, Jerez de la Frontera, Málaga and Seville – plus the 'offshore' option of flights into Gibraltar. Málaga is by far the easiest international option, with flights from around Europe, North Africa and North American hub airports, as well as international connections via Madrid. Both Seville and Granada have regular international services, and Almería is expanding its network of air connections. Spain's national airline **Iberia** (*tel: 902 400 500; (UK) 0870 609 0500; www.iberia.es*) operates national and international routes out of them all.

Seville's **San Pablo** airport (*tel: 954 44 99 00*) is 12km (7 miles) northeast of the city and a simple journey by car, taxi or bus (*half-hourly*) to the centre. Buses stop at **Santa Justa** railway station, which has connections to all Andalucían cities and most towns (*see p182*).

Málaga's **Pablo Ruiz Picasso** airport (*tel: 952 24 88 04*) is 8km (5 miles) west of the city and the most easily accessible of all Andalucían airports. As well as taxis and buses (*half-hourly*) there is also a handy suburban train connection just a few minutes' walk from the airport and signed from the arrivals and departures halls. This line, the Málaga–Fuengirola line, has a half-hourly service in both directions (*pay on board*). Anyone wanting to travel onwards by bus or train should get off at Estación RENFE, one stop before the terminus at Centro/Alameda, as advised by the automatic announcements on the train. The Málaga–Fuengirola station is below the main RENFE station here, and both are a short walk away from the Estación de Autobuses.

Some UK budget airlines have regular flights to Andalucía. Ryanair (*www.ryanair.com*) flies to Málaga, Granada, Almería, Seville and Jerez de la Frontera. easyJet (*www.easyjet.com*) flies to Almería and Málaga. Thomas Cook (*www.flythomascook.com*) organises flights to Almería, Jerez and Málaga.

By car
Visiting Seville and Andalucía from abroad by car is more an adventure than

Estación RENFE, Málaga

a comfortable option, but it is possible. Seville is roughly 600km (373 miles) from Spain's northern and southern borders with France, and a day's drive from Barcelona, Bilbao or Santander, which have handy ferry links to Britain (the last two being ports). For details of ferry services consult the *Thomas Cook European Rail Timetable* (*see p183 for details*).

Driving
The best map (*see pp185, 187, Maps*) to negotiate Andalucía by any form of transport is the Michelin: Andalucía 1/400,000. Many first-time visitors to Andalucía are surprised at how mountainous much of it is, and although many of the roads are excellent this fact should be borne in mind when hiring and driving cars here. Similarly, a special warning has to be issued about the N340, the *autovia* (motorway) that skirts Andalucía's coastline. It is said to be the most dangerous motorway in Europe.

The Spanish drive on the right, along with most continental Europeans. Traffic offences can lead to on-the-spot fines and the police may even accompany you to an ATM. Seatbelt use is obligatory. Speed limits are 120km/h (75mph) on *autovias* (motorways), 90km/h (56mph) on other roads and 50km/h (31mph) in built-up areas. *Bandas de sonoras* (speed bumps) are common in residential areas. Drink-driving is forbidden. Check cover for accident, theft of vehicle and liability with your travel insurer.

Petrol (*gasolina*) is available from *gasolineras* (petrol stations) as *super* (leaded), *sin plomo* (unleaded) and *gasoil* (diesel). *Gasolineras* are plentiful in and on the outskirts of cities and towns, but grow scarce in the more remote countryside.

Car hire

You will need to produce your passport and an EU or international driving licence to hire a car in Spain. The law requires that all cars carry a red warning triangle, replacement headlight bulbs – and a reflective yellow jacket for roadside emergencies.

International companies such as **Avis** (*tel: 902 13 55 31; www.avis.es*), **Europcar** (*tel: 913 43 45 12; www.europcar*) and **Hertz** (*tel: 902 40 24 05; www.hertz.es*) have offices at all airports and in most city and town centres.

It is invariably cheaper and more convenient to pre-pay your car hire before you leave your country of departure.

By coach

Coach (*autobus*) is the most popular and cheapest form of transport in Spain. These services are more frequent than trains and reach far more destinations.

Estaciónes de autobuses are commonly found (and signed) on the perimeter of the city centre, such as Seville's Prado de San Sebastián (*tel: 954 41 71 11*) for southbound buses, and Plaza des Armas (*tel: 954 90 77 37*) for westbound services. The bus system is privatised, with as many as six or more different companies operating different routes, and they vary from city to city and town to town.

Pre-booking is possible only at bus stations and it is common to pay on board for all but long-distance routes. Be warned that bus services around weekends are often pre-booked by students returning home and families on the move.

By train

With sufficient time on your hands, trains are the most comfortable and scenic way to explore Andalucía. It is even possible to visit from northern Europe, although an average journey from London or Paris would take two days.

Seville's **Santa Justa** railway station (*tel: 954 41 41 11*) sits at the centre of Andalucía's rail network. It's advisable to book ahead for any journeys between cities, particularly in summertime.

If pre-booking is not possible, leave plenty of time to purchase a ticket at the station. Anyone planning to travel around Andalucía should also check services and availability before making any firm plans involving train travel. Spain's RENFE (Red Nacíonal de Ferrocarilles Españoles) has a website (*www.renfe.es*) with information in Spanish and English, and a phone line (*tel: 902 24 02 02*). The phone line is Spanish, but there are operators fluent in English and other languages. Major travel agencies, Halcon Viajes and Viajes Marsans, have offices in all cities and towns and deal with domestic rail and coach travel as well as holidays abroad. A good company to advise you and make bookings before leaving home is Rail Europe (*tel: 08708 371 371; www.raileurope.com*).

The *Thomas Cook European Rail Timetable* is published monthly and gives up-to-date details of rail services and many ferry services throughout Europe; this will help you plan your journey to Spain and around Andalucia. It is available to buy online from *www.thomascookpublishing.com*, any branch of Thomas Cook in the UK or *tel: 01733 416477*.

Children

Children under four travel free on public transport. Young children in hotels often stay free, and older children at reduced rates, while family rooms with three or more beds are common in most hotels. Entry to state-owned museums is often free to under-18s, although some charge youth/student rates. There are sometimes reductions for under-12s, and special student rates for certain galleries, museums and concert halls.

Climate

Generally the east of Andalucía is much drier than the west with parts of Almería being desert. Although parts of the region get cold in winter and snow falls on the Sierra Nevada, on the coast it is possible to have breakfast outside in January. But as anywhere in the world these days, dramatic inversions of the climatic pattern are to be expected. Most commonly, Andalucía remains dry between May and September, with temperatures in the 20–30°C (70–90°F) range. Apart from the interior of Almería province and *el sartén* (the 'frying pan'), around Écija east of Seville, temperatures rarely rise above 38°C (100°F), and this

is usually a dry heat. Autumn weather becomes unpredictable around late October, and the best advice to travellers packing with weather in mind is to take layers of clothing and a waterproof. If you are travelling from the coast into the interior and/or mountains, expect a temperature drop of 6°C (10°F) or more.

Crime

Crime is as common in Andalucía as it is in northern Europe. Most crimes are opportunistic, and Seville and Granada are known for the frequency of car break-ins and random bag snatches. However, commonsense behaviour with vehicles, valuables and personal safety should protect the visitor against all but the most unfortunate incidents. Park in secured pay parking or hotel car parks where possible, and remove all your valuables whenever and wherever you park. Don't carry expensive valuables around with you, and take care of

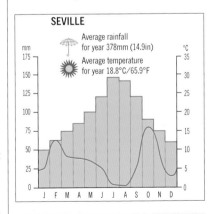

SEVILLE

Average rainfall for year 378mm (14.9in)

Average temperature for year 18.8°C/65.9°F

Weather Conversion Chart
25.4mm = 1 inch
°F = 1.8 x °C + 32

obvious targets such as cameras and bags.

It is important, however, to maintain a sense of perspective: you are no more likely to be robbed or attacked here than anywhere else in Europe, and certainly less than in any large North American city. Serious crimes are rare. If you are the victim of a crime, report it to the police as soon as possible, and enlist the assistance of hotels and others if possible.

Customs regulations

The duty-free allowance for EU visitors to Spain is: 800 cigarettes or 200 cigars, 10 litres of spirits or 90 litres of wine or 20 litres of fortified wine, 110 litres of beer, 60 centilitres of perfume and 250 centilitres of toilet water. Non-EU visitors should check with their embassy. There is no limit on the amount of money you may bring into Spain, although if you bring in large sums of cash, some way beyond expected living costs and likely purchases, you may be required by customs to prove that it is legal tender.

Documents and insurance

Tourists need to carry their passport or national identity card with them at all times. Drivers should always ensure that they have their car papers with them.

Embassies and consulates

Almost every country has an embassy or consulate in Spain, usually in Madrid. Some, such as Britain, also have consulates in Fuengirola, Málaga and Seville. Depending on your particular enquiry, it may be best to try Madrid before contacting a local office.

Conversion Table		
FROM	TO	MULTIPLY BY
Inches	Centimetres	2.54
Feet	Metres	0.3048
Yards	Metres	0.9144
Miles	Kilometres	1.6090
Acres	Hectares	0.4047
Gallons	Litres	4.5460
Ounces	Grams	28.35
Pounds	Grams	453.6
Pounds	Kilograms	0.4536
Tons	Tonnes	1.0160

To convert back, for example from centimetres to inches, divide by the number in the third column.

Men's Suits

UK		36	38	40	42	44	46	48
Rest of Europe	46	48	50	52	54	56	58
US		36	38	40	42	44	46	48

Dress Sizes

UK		8	10	12	14	16	18
France	36	38	40	42	44	46
Italy	38	40	42	44	46	48
Rest of Europe	34	36	38	40	42	44
US		6	8	10	12	14	16

Men's Shirts

UK	14	14.5	15	15.5	16	16.5	17
Rest of Europe	36	37	38	39/40	41	42	43
US	14	14.5	15	15.5	16	16.5	17

Men's Shoes

UK	7	7.5	8.5		9.5	10.5	11
Rest of Europe	41	42	43	44	45	46
US	8	8.5	9.5	10.5	11.5	12

Women's Shoes

UK	4.5	5	5.5	6	6.5	7
Rest of Europe	38	38	39	39	40	41
US	6	6.5	7	7.5	8	8.5

Embassies
Australia *Plaza del Descubridor, Diego Ordás 3, Madrid. Tel: 913 53 66 00; www.embaustralia.es*
Canada *Nuñez de Balboa 35, Madrid. Tel: 912 23 32 50; www.canada-es.org*
UK *Fernando el Santo 16, Madrid. Tel: 913 19 02 00; www.ukinspain.com*
USA *Serrano 75, Madrid. Tel: 915 87 22 00; www.embusa.es*

Consulates
Australia *calle Federico Rubio 14, Seville. Tel: 954 22 09 71.*
Canada *Edificio Horizonte, Plaza Malagueta 2, Málaga. Tel: 952 22 33 46.*
Ireland *Galerias Santa Monica, Avenida Boliches 15, Fuengirola. Tel: 952 47 51 08.*
UK *Edificio Eurocom, bloque Sur C/Mauricio Moro Pareto 2-2°, Málaga. Tel: 952 35 23 00.*
US *Plaza Nueva 8-8, 29 planta E2-4, Seville. Tel: 954 21 87 51.*

Emergency telephone numbers
Ambulance (*ambulancia*) *112*
Fire brigade (*bomberos*) *080*
General emergencies (*urgencias*) *112*
Police *092*
Medical emergencies (*doctor*) *061*

Health and insurance
EU citizens are entitled to free emergency treatment in Spain, but some non-urgent treatments are only available privately, which is why it is important for all visitors to Spain to arrange private travel insurance to cover treatment and the costs of repatriation. For British visitors, the European Health Insurance Card (EHIC) will cover most eventualities, but some treatments may require payment which can be claimed back later. Non-urgent cases can be dealt with at a local Centro de Salud during surgery hours. The EHIC is available from *www.ehic.org.uk*, by phoning *0845 606 2030* or from post offices.

There are no vaccine requirements to enter Spain.

Chemists
There is always one *farmacia* (chemist) open 24 hours a day in any district of a city and in most large towns, identified by a green cross above the entrance. Other chemists will display the address of the open *farmacia* when they are closed. Chemists are allowed to diagnose minor ailments and prescribe certain over-the-counter drugs to treat these. Not all over-the-counter drugs (antihistamines, for example) are as freely available in Spain as elsewhere.

Hostels and camping
There are youth hostels for students and backpackers in most of the main cities of Andalucia (Seville, Granada, Málaga, Almería, Huelva and Jerez de la Frontera), and also in Marbella, Sierra Nevada and Cazorla. For further information about youth hostels in Andalucia contact the **Red Española de Albergues Juveniles** (*www.reaj.com*).

The climate in Andalucia is usually good for camping. For visiting Málaga and the Costa del Sol there is a campsite in Marbella and another one in Ronda. South of Granada there is one site in Sierra Nevada and three in the Alpujarras (in Órgiva and Pitres), and near the sea there are two in Motril. The coast of Almería has a few camping

LANGUAGE

Many people working in hotels and restaurants will want to practise their English on you, but any attempt to speak Spanish will win you friends among the Spanish. Although in some respects it is a more complicated language than English, in one respect it is easier: words are pronounced as they look, according to a few simple rules.

PRONUNCIATION

Generally the accent falls on the second-to-last syllable unless it is marked with a written accent.

Vowel sounds

Vowels are always pronounced in the same way:

a	ah	o	oh
e	eh	u	oo
i	ee		

Consonant sounds

Consonants are the same as in English with the following exceptions:

ll like 'y' in 'yes'

rr is rolled, as in Scotland

h is silent

j like a guttural 'h'

g followed by 'e' or 'i' like a guttural 'h'

ñ like 'nio' as in 'onion'

v often sounds like a 'b'

USEFUL WORDS AND PHRASES

yes	si
no	no
please	por favor
thank you	gracias
you are welcome	de nada
bon appetit	buen provecho
hello	hola
goodbye	adiós
morning	mañana
good morning	buenos días
afternoon/evening	tarde
good afternoon/ good evening	buenas tardes
night	noche
good night	buenas noches
cheap	barato
expensive	caro
near	cerca
far	lejos
day	dia
week	semana
month	mes
year	año

NUMBERS

1	uno
2	dos
3	tres
4	cuatro
5	cinco
6	seis
7	siete
8	ocho
9	nueve
10	diez

DAYS OF THE WEEK

Sunday	domingo
Monday	lunes
Tuesday	martes
Wednesday	miércoles
Thursday	jueves
Friday	viernes
Saturday	sábado

sites in Mojácar, Cabo de Gata and Roquetas de Mar.

For nature lovers there is a campsite in the Sierra de Cazorla (in Jaén province), but for visiting Seville there is only one location near Alcalá de Guadaira. Cádiz, on the other hand, has a selection of campsites near the coast in San Roque, Tarifa and Zahara de los Atunes. For further information about camping in Andalucía, contact the **Federación Española de Empresarios de Campings** (*www.fedcamping.com*).

Maps

Tourist information offices distribute good free maps of their respective towns and cities. The best map shop in Andalucía is in the centre of Seville: **LTC** (*Avenida Menéndez Pelayo 42; tel: 954 42 59 64; www.ltcideas.com*), just beyond the Jardines de Murillo behind the Alcázar. In Britain, **Stanfords** (*12–14 Long Acre, WC2; tel: 020 7836 1321; www.stanfords.co.uk*) has branches in Bristol and Manchester. In Australia, try **Mapland** (*372 Little Bourke St; tel: 03 96 70 43 83; www.mapland.com.au*) in Melbourne; and in the United States **Traveler's Choice** (*2 Wooster St, NY; tel: 212 941 1535; email: tvlchoice@aol.com*).

Media

Most international editions of British, continental European and US newspapers such as the *Wall Street Journal* and *Herald Tribune* are available on the day of publication in Seville and other larger cities and towns. Most larger and more upmarket hotels have satellite television with at least one channel in English, French and German.

Public holidays

Some public holidays are celebrated all over Spain; others are confined to

Each town and village has a *centro de salud*, health centre, that can help with emergencies

Andalucía. In addition, every village, town and city has its own public holidays during the year.

1 January Año Nuevo (New Year's Day)
6 January Día de los Reyes (Epiphany)
28 February Día de Andalucía (regional holiday)
March or April (variable) Viernes Santo (Good Friday)
1 May Día del Trabajo (Labour Day)
15 August Asunción de la Virgen (Assumption of the Blessed Virgin Mary)
12 October Día de la Hispanidad (National Day of Spain)
1 November Todos los Santos (All Saints' Day)
6 December Día de la Constitución (Constitution Day)
8 December Inmaculada Concepción (Immaculate Conception)
25 December Día de Navidad (Christmas Day)

Sustainable tourism

Thomas Cook is a strong advocate of ethical and fairly traded tourism and believes that the travel experience should be as good for the places visited as it is for the people who visit them. That's why we firmly support The Travel Foundation, a charity that develops solutions to help improve and protect holiday destinations, their environment,

Cities and most large towns will have a *kiosco*, or newsstand, stocking international publications

traditions and culture. To find out what you can do to make a positive difference to the places you travel to and the people who live there, please visit *www.thetravelfoundation.org.uk*

Time
Spain follows Central European Time, which is GMT (Greenwich Mean Time) plus one hour, or US EST (Eastern Standard Time) plus six hours.

Toilets
Public toilets are a rarity in Andalucía, as in the rest of Spain, although all department stores and public monuments have them. A café or bar is the best alternative. It is polite to buy a drink when making use of the facilities.

Tourist information
The responsibility for providing tourist information in Spain has been devolved to the regions, which in turn have devolved resources to each town and city. This makes it frustratingly difficult to get good information in advance of your visit, and so your best source is always the tourist information office on the spot. There are information posts at the major airports and railway stations.

Two good places to start planning a visit to Andalucía are Spain's national tourist website *www.spain.info* and the website of the regional government (Junta de Andalucía) *www.andalucía.org.* The Junta de Andalucía maintains a network of tourist information offices in the major cities, but some of them have a sparse supply of leaflets, which, bizarrely, they charge for. Another useful, privately-run site is *www.andalucía.com*

Seville's main tourist information office is at Plaza de San Francisco 19, next to the city hall (*tel: 954 59 52 88; www.turismo.sevilla.org*). For information about Granada, see *www.granadatur.com*, and for Córdoba, see *www.turismodecordoba.org*

There are cashpoint machines in most towns

ACKNOWLEDGEMENTS

Thomas Cook Publishing wishes to thank the photographers, picture libraries and other organisations for the loan of the photographs reproduced in this book, to whom the copyright in the photographs belong.

NICK INMAN 2, 5, 36, 37, 39, 46, 47, 48, 49, 77, 92, 93, 98, 99, 120, 135, 139, 140, 141, 149, 152a, 155, 161, 165, 166, 168; NICK STUBBS 105, 125; WORLD PICTURES 1, 19, 79, 97, 129, 160, 172; GRAN TEATRO DE CORDOBA 159; HOTEL ACINIPO 174

The remaining pictures were supplied by MICHELLE CHAPLOW/ANDALUCÍA SLIDE LIBRARY.

Copy-editing: KATY CARTER

Index: INDEXING SPECIALISTS (UK) LTD

Maps: IFA DESIGN LTD, Plymouth, UK

Proof-reading: CAMBRIDGE PUBLISHING MANAGEMENT LTD

Send your thoughts to
books@thomascook.com

We're committed to providing the very best up-to-date information in our travel guides and constantly strive to make them as useful as they can be. You can help us to improve future editions by letting us have your feedback. If you've made a wonderful discovery on your travels that we don't already feature, if you'd like to inform us about recent changes to anything that we do include, or if you simply want to let us know your thoughts about this guidebook and how we can make it even better – we'd love to hear from you.

Send us ideas, discoveries and recommendations today and then look out for your valuable input in the next edition of this title. And, as an extra 'thank you' from Thomas Cook Publishing, you'll be automatically entered into our exciting monthly prize draw.

Emails to the above address, or letters to Travellers Project Editor, Thomas Cook Publishing, PO Box 227, Unit 18, Coningsby Road, Peterborough PE3 8SB, UK.

Please don't forget to let us know which title your feedback refers to!